Pinal Dave

Pinal is an eternal learner and avid technology blogger. He has authored 11 books and built 15 e-learning video courses with Pluralsight. He has been a part of the IT industry for more than ten years and works for Pluralsight. He received his Master of Science from the University of Southern California and a Bachelors of Engineering from Gujarat University. Additionally, he holds many Microsoft certificates.

Pinal writes every day on his blog http://blog.sqlauthority.com for over 8 years on various subjects concerning SQL, NoSQL, and Business Intelligence. His blog has over million visitors every month and he is known for engaging users with his skills of explaining a complex subject in simple words. When he is not in front of a computer, he is usually travelling to explore hidden treasures in nature with his daughter, Shaivi, and very supportive wife, Nupur.

Jillian Gile

Jillian has been writing and editing blogs for five years. She currently is a freelance writer and a guest blogger for a variety of websites. She has her Master of Science in Biology from Washington State Univerisity. When Jillian is not writing, she is a Research Scientist for the Univeristy of Washington.

Secret Tool Box of Box of Successful Bloggers

52 Tips to Build a High Traffic Top Ranking Blog

This book is dedicated to

Aaron Skonnard

An eternal optimist, truth seeker and entrepreneur.

His mission to democratize the learning is bringing future, fortune and freedom to technology professionals all around the world – knowingly and unknowingly.

The most useful piece of learning for the uses of life is to unlearn what is untrue. ~ Antisth

Author's Foreword

We all love to express ourselves and blogging is a great medium for the same. Before this book I have published 11 technology books. This is my first non-technical book based on my 8+ experience of running a large scale successful blog. I tried to make this book as thorough and complete as possible, knowing that in the world of blogging, nothing stays up-to-date for very long.

So it is with great pleasure that I introduce a new blogging book! This book is going to focus on how to be the "Best Blogger" you can be – whether you are new, experienced, or just curious. The goal of this book is to cover the highlights, interesting new topics, and questions that I received after my courses. There is no way to become an "encyclopedia" of blogging, but I am going to try to be entertaining and informative, at least.

The format of this book will be one topic per chapter, with 52 topics. If you would like, you can read one chapter a week, so it will be a whole year of learning. If you are like me, though, once you start learning you don't want to stop, so you can finish this book quickly!

I have never in my life learned anything from any man who agreed with me.

~ Dudley Field Malone

Contents

Chapter 1 - Introduction

Welcome!

This introductory chapter will count as #1, so if you are reading this, welcome to the new blogging course! I don't want to give away too many of the secrets we all are going to learn, but here is a quick glimpse at what we have in store:

How to Start a Blog

If anyone out there has ever tried to start a blog, you know that the stereotype is almost the hardest part. Figuring out how to post, where to post, and what to post is like trying to drink out of a fire hose. Once you have chosen one of the millions of options, sitting down to write every day feels easy. I want to make the whole thing easy!

How to Design a Blog

This topic is probably going to stretch over many posts. Unfortunately, it is very common that a blogger has a lot of good things to say, but no one pays attention because his or her website looks cheap, spammy, or is just hard to find.

What to Write

I said earlier that starting the blog is the hardest part, and writing is the easy part. Well, this is all relative, because the day is going to come when you sit and stare at your computer screen with no words to say. I hope I have a lot to say about to break Writer's Block!

To Comment or Not to Comment

Comments can be the heart and soul of a blog – or they can be a dark, scary alley way where trolls hide and spammers flood the comments section with advertisements. Choosing whether to allow comments, how to monitor comments, and what to say on other people's blogs deserves its own week (if not month!).

Monetizing a Blog

There is a saying that when you do what you love, you'll never work a day in your life. If you love blogging, you might want to turn it into your career – and I hope to show at least a few of you how to do it.

I hope you all are just as excited as I am to start this new adventure!

Tip from Pinal -

Read one chapter once a week and implement it every day. You will have an amazing blog one year from now.

Chapter 2 - How To Start a Blog

I spent a lot of time wondering what to write about in this "inaugural" chapter of the book. There are a lot of things to keep in mind when you start blogging, and it was hard to determine if I should write for the experts or the rookies. In fact, starting this book was almost as hard as starting a blog!

And that's what made me decide to start with this topic. Maybe you have been wondering if you should start blogging, maybe you are an expert with multiple successful blogs but are interested in starting another. Maybe blogging has been a dream of yours, but there is a road block stopping you. I believe everyone can use some advice and a helping hand when it comes to starting a blog.

There are a lot of things to consider when you're just beginning, but let me make it easy: just start writing. Even if you are just writing down ideas and outlines in a notebook, consider this the foundation of your blog. You have laid the groundwork already, congratulations!

The second thing is: get your blog online. Choose a blogging platform and get going. Yes, there are a lot of options to choose from, which we will cover in detail in the next post, so for now, just pick one and go! This choice is not set in stone – you can always switch later. The top choices are: WordPress, Blogger, TypePad, and some of the other "microblogs," like Tumblr or Twitter. If you will be writing on a highly specialized or technical topic, you can also check out if your field has a dedicated or preferred platform.

For the first 10 days, try to write at least once a day. Blogs don't tend to appear on search engines until there are about 10 posts, but dumping 10 posts straight onto a blog looks a lot like spam to a search engine, so try to post something once a day (this will also give new readers a nice chunk to dive into). Once you start this habit, keep it up! It no longer has to be once a day, but keep a regular schedule or, like a New Year's resolution, this habit will fall by the wayside, too.

Before you know it, you have a blog up and running – it really is that simple. Later on we will look at topics like blog design, commenting, and monetizing your blog – but you can't worry about things like that without a blog to put them on, so starting up is the first step in your journey of a thousand miles.

Tip from Jill -

Start steady and consistently, it helps you to rank better with search engines and builds habit.

Chapter 3 - Choosing a Blogging Platform

Choosing a blogging platform can be extremely daunting. It can be like going to the store to buy toothpaste, and then being unable to decide between the 100 different kinds. Except with a blog, you are dedicated to this "toothpaste" for a lifetime, and it will follow you around and possibly haunt you the rest of your life. That's not scary at all, right?

To help you choose which platform to use, think about what kind of blog you envision for yourself, and how you will be using it. Do you want to post lots of pictures with very little text? Do you want your writing to shine, and your blog to have a "newspaper" feel (lots of text, few pictures)? Is your "brand" most important to you, and you want your name to be popular and catchy?

If you want to become your own brand or stand out from the blogging crowd, having your own domain name (yourname.com vs. yourname.blog-platform.com) may be very important to you. In these situations, I always recommend WordPress. It is free, easy to use as any other platform, and allows users to transition to a "branded" domain name (yourname.com) rather than one that is yourname.WordPress.com.

Other considerations – how comfortable do you feel with HTML coding? Many blog platforms will take this completely out of your hands, and your whole design is based on templates provided by the platform. If you know nothing about coding, this is obviously the way to go. Blogger tends to be the favorite for non-coders, it provides many different themes, but very few plug-ins. WordPress and TypePad both have no-code options, but WordPress leads the pack with plug-in options and themes.

If you want your own unique theme, you will have to learn to code, or hire someone who does. WordPress and TypePad both support this option, but keep in mind that TypePad has a small fee (less than $10) that will have to be factored into the overall costs.

As you can tell, Blogger, WordPress, and TypePad are the three leaders in blogging platforms. Give each a trial run, look at blogs that run on these platforms, and read reviews. Find the one you are most comfortable with – if you find the perfect theme and plug-in for your site, there is no need to go with the platform that has 1500 others. While I did say that choosing a platform can be like getting stuck with one brand of toothpaste for life, that is not always the case – more on that later.

Tip from Pinal -

Choose a blogging platform which lets you customize your template, as it is very crucial for a successful blog.

Chapter 4 - How Often to Post

So, you have a blog – now what? You might feel like you just brought home a new puppy (or a new baby). It might feel completely overwhelming and you're not sure what to do with it yet, but you know you're excited. Here is what to do next: start writing!

Even if your blog is meant to be focused on photographs and images, you're going to have to create content for your blog. If your blog is all technical talk, you're *definitely* going to need content. So start writing!

I have said it twice now, with two exclamation marks, to show how serious I am. In the first few hours of your blog's life, you really should create 10 posts to put up on your blog. Don't dump them there all at once – it will make search engines think your blog is very spammy – but have them ready to go up bright and early first thing every day for ten days in a row (or even spaced 12 hours apart, two a day). Search engines can be touchy creatures – they don't want you to dump your posts online, but the rule of thumb is they also won't recognize your blog until there are 10 posts. More readers than you think will find your blog through a simple Google search, so you want Google to be your friend.

I feel like we have covered the "10 post" rule for now. It is important. Don't forget it. But once you have finished the 10-post hump, it is important to keep up the momentum. In the first place, the more posts on your blog, the more legitimate it will look, and as I mentioned before, it will make search engine spiders your friend. In the second place, posts are the life blood of a blog. If three days go between posts, your readers will understand (unless your blog is about timely news or celebrity gossip). If three months go by between posts, your readership will all but dry up. This goes for text blogs and photo blogs, and everything in between.

As with most blogging advice – the exact details are a personal choice. You may want to post something seven days a week, 365 days a year. This can be a hard pace to keep up, but if that is the speed your blog needs, it can be done. Many bloggers aim for once a week, or a few times a week. Some do not give themselves deadlines, and post every day or once a week, whatever feels best to them.

The best advice I can give is – have fun! You have a brand new blog, and alike a new puppy or a new baby, enjoy every moment and make sure you're leaving good memories.

Tip from Jill -

Frequency of blogging should not impact the quality of your blog. A regular calendar of blog posts improves traffic and loyal readership.

Chapter 5 - How Many Authors Does a Blog Need?

When you think a blog, what do you picture? Probably a page, with five to 10 posts, each five to 10 paragraphs long. You might have a favorite blog in mind, and are picturing its layout, logo, and author photo. I'd like you to think really hard about that author photo right now.

Chances are you are picturing one individual. A majority of blogs are single author enterprises. But you might be surprised if you take a look at the author information for some blogs. Many more than you'd think having multiple authors, contributors, or special guests who post on a regular basis.

If you are a blogger yourself, thinking about becoming a multi-author can be worth considering. Obviously, if the point of your blog is to air your own personal opinions, bringing in another author would be completely counterintuitive. If your goals are to create the strongest blog on a certain topic, having multiple opinions and help churning out frequent posts can be a huge plus.

There are definitely downsides to sharing the credit on a blog. The first of which is, of course, sharing the credit!   However, I think multiple authors is something than many bloggers are completely unaware of, let alone one that they have seriously considered, and I'd like to say right now that it is worth considering.

Reason one – the day may come when you need help creating content. You might be completely burned out, or having nothing to say on a topic, or maybe you just want to go on vacation without building up a backlog of posts in advance. Sometimes everyone needs a hand.

Reason two – having a second opinion makes any argument well-rounded, and the same is true of blogs. Maybe the back-and-forth of two different voices will be what makes your blog a must-read. Maybe you just want to argue with your best friend in a public forum. Whatever your reasons, it's worth considering.

Reason three – A second, third, fourth voice can be like a breath of fresh air. The more voices on your blog, the fresher it will sound. Depending on the topic you're all talking about, it can make your blog very strong.

This topic is going to end much like many of my others – in the end, having multiple authors is a personal choice. If it doesn't work for your blog, that is fine, but I did want to give some bloggers the option to consider. And if you're tempted but don't want to bring someone in permanently, guest posting is always an option, which we'll learn about next time.

Tip from Pinal -

Blogging might seem like a solo activity, but you can definitely start a blog with a co-author, an occasional author, or just invite guest posters.

Chapter 6 - Guest Posts

We have recently discussed multiple author blogs, and how they are an often-overlooked option. If it was something that intrigued you, or even something that completely turned you away, please stop and consider guest posting now.

Guest posting is a pretty easy concept – you invite another person, well-known or not, to author one post, a series of posts, or maybe a recurring series on your blog. There is also the option of becoming a guest poster on someone else's blog. Both of these options have a lot of perks and very few drawbacks.

Having a guest on your blog can be great. It can be a breath of fresh air, and it can give you a much-needed break. You can find an expert on a topic that you are not too sure about, and it can make you a lot of good contacts in the blogging world. If your guest is a well-known individual, it can also gain you access to a whole new set of readers.

So where do you find a guest blogger? The first step is to ask. Ask a friend, a neighbor, the blogger who you are a devoted reader of. Maybe you can find a social network connection (LinkedIn, Facebook) whose opinion you'd like to hear, or a message board you frequent has an especially active member. The great thing about guest blogging is that you present the person's credentials, and your readers will automatically trust you. You don't have to act like a national news anchor, vetting every visitor and opinion. If the idea of a guest poster makes you nervous, remember that you will have the first read-through of the post and final say about whether it appears on your blog or not.

On the other hand, how do you become a guest blogger for someone else? It is a very similar thing. Keep your eyes open for offers of guest posts on blogs, social networks, or message boards. You can even try a "cold call" technique and send e-mails to blogs you'd like to be a guest of, with an outline or rough draft of what your post would be. The worst thing that can happen is they might say no – nothing ventured, nothing gained.

Becoming a guest blogger is also a good way to get your name and your blog out there. If you really pique a reader's interest, they might even follow your link to your blog and become a regular reader. Becoming a popular (and well-paid) blogger is all about name recognition, and guest blogging can only help your cause.

Obviously, if you don't feel guest blogging is right for you or your blog, it is not an extreme necessity. But it is definitely something to consider, especially if you love blogs and blogging – why not do as much as you can?

Tip from Jill -

Guest posting can bring new readers to your blog, and get your name out there on other blogs. It is basically free publicity!

Chapter 7 - What to Write – An Introduction

We have previously discussed how important it is to write posts regularly, and that frequent, regular posts are the lifeblood of blogs. It is easy for me to sit here and say – writing is important! Write more! But now I want to back up my words, and really get into *how* to write a blog post.

So why talk about something so basic? Maybe you are a new blogger, or not a strong writer, or have run into writer's block. Maybe you are a veteran blogger, but you feel like your posts could use some help, or lack something. No matter where you are in the blogging stage, it is always important to look at the building blocks and see what there is to learn.

So let's start at the very beginning: The Introduction. This might be sounding like a Writing 101 class, and that is the way it is meant to be. When you start writing anything, you should probably start at the beginning. Sometimes it can be catchy to begin a story in the middle and work backwards, but let's consider that Masters-level writing, and think about just the intro right now.

The first paragraph of your blog should introduce the topic you're about to talk about. It can even say: "I am going to talk about XYZ." Blogs don't need to be an exercise in the next Great Novel, so there is no need to be fancy and start with a flashback or other fancy exercises.

Of course, you don't necessarily have to say, "I am going to talk about XYZ." Let's face it, that can be a little boring. You can start by talking about a metaphor – some readers might remember my comparison of choosing a blog platform to choosing a toothpaste.

You can also start a blog post with a story – as long as it is related to the rest of the post, of course. For a complex topic, you might even need to introduce the introduction, sort of like what I did with this exact post. I had to introduce the idea of writing, and how to write, and then talk about how to introduce a blog.

Obviously there are many different ways to go about it, and if you are feeling questionable about how well your blog post is going, have someone else read it. If there is any confusion, their first question and your first answer will probably help you write your introduction!

Tip from Pinal -

The first sentence can be the hardest part of writing the whole blog post! There are many ways to break the writer's block, but the easiest is just to say "I am going to talk about XYZ."

Chapter 8 - What to Write – Topics

In the last chapter, we discussed introducing your blog. Let's move on to a new building block of blog writing – choosing a topic. If you have a very thematic blog, about a very specific field, you might be thinking – I have my topics planned out for a lifetime! There will never be a need to sit and think, "what should I write?" Don't get too smug – writer's block can hit anyone. I do not say this to be mean, I just want to be honest with all my readers.

No matter what your blog is about, at some point you will probably get tired of writing the same old wrap up of new and breaking news. You will get tired of writing long opinion posts. If you write the same sort of post every single day, you are *going* to get tired of it. So let me finally start talking about the different types of topics you can cover.

I just mentioned these: breaking news and opinions. These topics, no matter your field, are always going to make great posts. Even if you don't stay up reading websites for the latest news, your readers will still like to hear your take on them.

Try the ever-popular list. "Top Five XYX," "Best Ten ABC," "Twelve Things To Remember," "Fifteen Things to Forget." If you do these every day for weeks or months, your readers might stop taking you seriously, but they can be really great for shaking things up.

Pick a picture and talk about it. Yes, this sounds a little silly, especially if you have a very technical blog, but you might be amazed at the kind of discussions and philosophy one good picture can elicit.

Host a contest. This will generate you not just one post, but at least THREE – the introduction, the collection of votes/ballots/entries (this a stretch into multiple posts), and the announcement of the winner. It can be a contest for anything, with as big or little a prize as you'd like.

Have your readers write your post for you. This sounds mean, but I am talking about introducing a topic for discussion, and then opening up the comments for your readers to tell you (and everyone else) what they think. This can work for almost any type of blog.

Have someone else write the post for you. This also sounds mean, but we have already discussed guest posts, and this is what I am talking about now. Think of it as doing a fellow blogger a favor, to get their name out there. Who knows, maybe you will guest post for someone and return the favor some day.

Tip from Jill -

Think you don't have anything to say? Think again! Write about a picture, write a "top five" list, host a contest. These are only a few ideas!

Chapter 9 - What to Write – Lists

In the last chapter, we briefly mentioned lists as a possible blog topic. Now I am going to expand on this topic because I think that lists are a highly undervalued area for exploration in blogs. Some authorities tend to consider them a "lesser" form of a blog post, and their arguments are valid.

Let me give the downsides first. Lists can seem juvenile and "cheap." They can be seen as the easy way out for lazy bloggers. Writer's block is no joke, and it can be easy to fall back on the easiness and the familiarity of lists. There are also many, many entertainment websites that have abused the power of lists – top ten movies, top ten pictures of kittens, top ten jokes, top ten celebrity photos. I could make a list of list-style blogs!

But with this said, lists certainly have their place on the average blog. They can act as a "placeholder" - a way to catch your breath and recharge for the next big post. My favorite way to use them is to introduce an upcoming series, with each item on the list becoming its own blog topic.

So, yes, list blog posts can be the easy way out of a hard situation. But that doesn't mean they are without worth. The important thing is thing is to use lists wisely, sparingly, and to the best effect. Let's go over how to do just that.

How to use a list wisely? Make sure you are writing important lists. If your blog is about gardening, don't discuss celebrity outfits. It is better to not produce a post at all than one that is bad quality. It is better to just announce you need a vacation in that situation. Don't make a list of old material, either, that is what the index of the blog is for. Many readers to back and read old posts, so there is no reason to waste their time with a summary post – unless there is a reason, of course, like a big anniversary or going over important building blocks for introducing a complex new subject.

The definition of using a chapter "sparingly," is open to interpretation, and everyone's needs will be different. For example, if you only have one post a month, using a list-style post once a month is too often. For most blogs, however, with multiple posts a week or daily, the "once a month" rule is probably okay.

I am a big fan of list posts – both writing and reading them. I think that most blogs can benefit from them, and you shouldn't be scared away by their reputation. If you follow the guidelines here, I think every blog can use list posts.

Tip from Pinal -

List posts can be a great way to get the creative juices flowing, and to capture the interest in readers. As long as you're not over-using the trick, they are a great option for posting.

Chapter 10 - What to Write – Discussions

To continue with our "what to write" theme, I would like to cover discussion posts right now. Discussion posts can come in plenty of styles, and there is no way I can cover each and every one of them right now, so let me cover the kind that I think most people will use, and that I find most effective.

The most basic type of discussion post is very simple, and only a few sentences long. It usually goes like this: I just read XYZ. What do you think about it? Then the comment section is open to comments from the readers. The blogger may or may not get involved with comments, moderating, or eventually adding to the post. If you have committed, involved readers, this kind of post is invaluable. If you don't know how many readers you have, if they are regulars or not, and your comments are usually just crickets chirping, this kind of post might not work for you.

Discussion posts can also be a little more structured. You can write a full-length post about the topic, your thoughts and opinions, and then the comment section might simply involve into a deep discussion amongst your readers. Sometimes you can predict these reactions, and sometimes the stars just align in the right way to get people talking. An easy way to get discussion going is to end your blog post with: "please discuss!"

One way to ensure that discussions happen on your blog is to make sure that your blog has a good comments section. First of all – make sure comments are enabled! This isn't always the default setting for most blog platforms. Secondly, moderate your comments. This can range anywhere from vetting each and every post before it goes online, approving commenters with good credentials, hovering over your comment section with a finger on the delete button, to using a commenting system that allows up-voting, down-voting, and flagging of inappropriate content. This is important to foster civil discussion as well as weeding out spammers who just want to sell diet drugs and dating websites.

I believe that good discussion is the lifeblood of a blog. It helps the blogger know people are reading and lively discussion can even generate future blog posts. Blogs with good comments can bring in readers looking for intelligent discussions and become a feature on its own beyond the great content created by the actual blogger. There are actually quite a few blogs that have grown to almost world-wide popularity based on the quality of their comments.

Even if this is not the future you want for your blog, or one that you believe is possible, it is something worth considering – if only to generate content for future posts!

Tip from Jill -

Discussion posts are some of the most thought provoking, but difficult posts to write. One way to add to the discussion is to allow commenting on your blog.

Chapter 11 - When Not to Write & What Not to Write

By now, you all probably know that I believe writing blog posts is the most important part of having a blog. Creating consistent content is definitely key. We have written quite a few chapters now about "what to write." So is there anything you *shouldn't* write?

Of course! That was a silly question. There is a little rule that I try to follow, not only on my blog, but in the rest of my life as well – don't say anything you wouldn't want to say in front of your grandmother. Your grandmother might not be at all interested in your blog or even the internet, but I still think this is a good rule to follow.

Nothing is going to ruin the reputation of your blog faster than the image that your blog is mean, vindictive, angry, unfair, or similar. Some controversy may bring in readers, but extended periods of anger and hate are going to drive ALL readers away. Before you hit "submit" on a new post, pause for just a minute and ask yourself if you are proud of all the content, or if there are bits you'd want censored before granny reads it. If there is anything questionable, maybe sleep on it and rethink posting it tomorrow morning.

After all, there are definitely times when a little bit of anger is necessary. Your opinion about developments in your field might not be all sunshine and butterflies. Most grandmas would understand this, and wouldn't mind reading your opinion on the matter. But personal attacks, unthinking comments, or biased opinions should probably be kept to yourself.

This brings me to another rule of thumb: don't write angry. This is sort of like the "don't drive angry" rule. If your emotions are taking control of your actions, you shouldn't be operating a dangerous motor vehicle, and you shouldn't be in control of a blog that has public readership, either. Chances are that whatever you write in the heat of the moment, you will regret the next morning. Writing while angry can kind of be like driving a car with no brakes.

So, if there is ever a question of what not to write and *when* not to write, I think the answer to both is the same – try not to write in anger. There is definitely a place on your blog for opinion and disagreements, but rage and fury tend not to make good reading.

By all means, write out exactly what you'd like to say to that person you disagree with, who made you angry, or who represents everything you hate. But do not post that article! Print out a copy and destroy the digital version to remove the temptation. The next day, take a look at what you wrote. Maybe you will be able to create a much better blog post out of it (maybe by simply taking out some of the meaner adjectives). But trust me, you will thank yourself later for not posting it immediately.

Tip from Pinal -

If you're not sure whether to post what you've written – ask yourself, "would I say this in front of my grandma?"

Chapter 12 - Contests

A few chapters ago, we talked briefly about using contests to gain publicity and readers. This is one of my favorite parts of writing a blog (and not just to gain publicity) so I'd like to write a little more about it right now.

Who doesn't love to give and receive presents? Being able to do something nice for a loved one is a reward in itself. If you are very lucky, you will come to feel the same way about your blog readers. They are always there for you, they leave interesting and supportive comments – it can feel a little bit like having your own fan club.

Contests, to me, are a way of giving back to the readers. Very few bloggers are going to be able to buy a present for every single reader, not only because it would cost a lot of money, but hopefully there are so many readers you couldn't afford to buy even a $1 present for all of them! Contests are a way to let readers know you care, and to be able to pick one or a few readers to benefit, while giving everyone a chance to win.

Contests are also going to have the benefit of drawing attention to your blog, and gaining you new readers if you are lucky. Everyone loves to win things, and they might visit your blog just for that opportunity. Then your wonderful writing style and interesting content will draw them in and they will become regular readers – that is the hope anyway!

So what can you give away in a contest? If you are blogging, you probably don't have $1 million to give away. Don't worry, the prizes are much different in the world of blogging. You can definitely give away some sort of cash or gift as a prize. Gift certificates work well and are easy to ship. Artwork can be a fun change, or you can provide a discount code to a service directly related to your blog (eBooks, computer programs, games, etc.

The contest can also be to allow readers to showcase some of their own work on your blog – this works especially well for more artistic-related blogs, where the contest winner (randomly selected, or chosen based on submitted work) can display their drawing, photograph, video, etc.

The more popular your blog gets, the more opportunity you will have to get sponsors for your contest from businesses interested in the market your readers represent. These can be good opportunities, although you might want to use them sparingly to avoid looking too commercial.

I think contests can work for any type of blog. If it seems scary, just remember that the stakes are much lower for a blog. No one is expecting to win the lottery!

Tip from Jill -

Contests are a lot of fun. They reward consistent readers and bring in new ones. You don't have to be Oprah to give away prizes!

Chapter 13 - Types of Contests

In the last chapter, we talked a little bit about what you can give away in a contest, and the short answer really is, "Anything!" We mentioned giving away physical items, or online perks. The prize in a contest is really the minor part – people see "contest" and want to participate. So – the prizes do not define the contest.

There are many *ways* to give away your prizes. The first way is to make the playing field even and a draw a name at random – out of a hat, out of a bowl, using a dartboard, whatever! The trick will be in how people submit their names. Many bloggers use the "leave a comment to enter the contest" tactic. If you have an active comment section and many regular commenters, this can be a great way to give back to your community.

You can also have people submit names via e-mail, which can work well for privacy issues or if you are having problems with your comments section (or would rather not have a comment section on your blog). You an also bring in social media – have people leave you a comment online, or "like" a Facebook post or photo, or use a special hashtag on Twitter. If you can think of a better way, by all means use it!

You can also have a "merit based" contest. This means that anyone who wants a chance to win the prize must submit something, and you judge which one is the best. This is a great way to tailor the contest to your blog – art, photographs, cooking, programming, anything! You can have people mail you a real sample, or leave a description in the comments, or send you a picture. The ways to gather these submissions are as varied as ways to pick a random winner.

Be warned – these kinds of contests are very hard to judge! You may find yourself giving consolation prizes to two, three, maybe ten people who you didn't want to hurt by rejection. On the upside, though, you can generate amazing content. Think of all the blog posts you will get by showing off your favorite submissions. This can also be a great way to give back to your community, by giving publicity to your fans.

The types of contests and ways to give away prizes are about as numerous as what your imagination can think up. I believe that contests are a great way to reward readers and to keep them coming back to your blog.

Tip from Pinal -

There are as many ways to choose a contest winner (or winners) as there are types of contest. The best advice I can give here – good luck!

Chapter 14 - Giveaways and Promotions

We've talked a little bit about contests, but if they don't sound like something you want on your blog, there are other ways to reward readers and give away free stuff. These are all great ways to gather new readers and show your appreciation for your current crowd.

One way to give stuff away is to just... give stuff away. You can choose the recipients any way you'd like, and you can choose the item to give away any way you'd like. There doesn't have to be any sort of competition or contest. It's something that many bloggers forget – it's their blog, they have the power.

You can also link these free giveaways to promotions. This is a way to advertise any product you'd like. Some people give away things that have their blog name and address on them – a way to promote their blog. Others give away things that have been sponsored by other companies – a way to earn a little money.

The ways to get promotions on your blog are about as numerous as the types of things to give away. If you just want to promote yourself, there are hundreds of companies that will emblazon your name and logo on just about anything – cups, hats, shirts, magnets, cars, you name it. You can find these companies on the internet or even in the "real world," and for a small fee, you can have piles of things to give away to your readers.

If you'd like to help out a fellow blogger or a company you'd like to support – just ask! Many websites have a "contact me" option, just shoot them an e-mail and say you'd like to give them a little free publicity on your blog (provide a link to your blog to prove you're legitimate, and maybe give a little info about your readership), and many times you will receive a quick response, including boxes of items to give away on your blog.

If you are very lucky, a company may actually contact you with an interest in reaching the market your readers represent. They may want to advertise to that particular niche regarding their product, and a way to get the word out – give away a free copy to the readers. They may even be willing to compensate you for the privilege. This is usually a good thing to reveal to your readers, though, to prevent any accusations that you have been "bought" or have no scruples about offering up your readers like bait.

The next step is the really fun part – giving stuff away! Everyone like receiving presents, and giving them to friends and loved ones can be almost as rewarding. You can decide how and when – it can almost feel like being Santa Claus!

Tip from Jill -

If you don't feel like hosting a contest, just giving free things to your readers is fine, too. It doesn't have to be big – and you can even get another company to provide the free stuff.

Chapter 15 - Cross-Blog Advertising

Writing a blog can be hugely rewarding. Think about it – you can turn your hobby or passion into a career. You get to write every day about something you really love and care about, you get to hear opinions from people who are interested in the same subject, and you can expand your community of like-minded people. Your blog can become an online community – a destination for people who care about the same thing and want to share their opinions.

Not only can your blog become a community, it can help you branch out and create an even larger community – among other bloggers, with friendships that might even grow out into the real world. Some people have a mental image of a blogger as a loner in a dark room, typing away at a glowing screen. The opposite is so often true! Bloggers may start out working alone on a passion project, but soon find themselves enmeshed in a lively, active community.

One of the perks of working in a community is the ability to help each other out. This can be for real-world issues like providing a room for someone to stay in, making a meal for someone who is hungry, or even helping out someone with their blog. We have already briefly discussed guest posting, and this is definitely something that blogging communities do for each other, but you also don't have to loan out your whole blog to a friend.

Cross-blog advertising is definitely a way to help out a fellow blogger, and get some help in return. This is basically self explanatory – your friend with a similar blog, post a link, icon, or full advertisement to your blog where their readers will see it, and it will gain you traffic and notoriety (the good kind). Of course, you will probably want to return the favor and post a similar advertisement about your friend's blog.

How will this help either of your blogs? Remember that community, we talked about – readers interested in a subject form a community of like-minded people. Well, often those people are looking for more blogs to find, more people to meet, more opinions to read. If you have a very popular blog with active readers, you can do your friend a favor by sending readers their way – and vice versa.

If you are a beginning blogger, don't be afraid to get involved in the community – even if you don't have a lot of fame or traffic. You never know when one of these contacts falls in love with what you do and offers to send a little business your way. Cross-blog advertising has no strict form or rules, but should be viewed as a big favor that is not bestowed lightly.

Tip from Pinal -

Blogging is a community, and one of the perks is cross-blog advertising.   It is not a task to be undertaken lightly, but the perks are tremendous.

Chapter 16 - Sponsored Posts

Let's face it, blogging can be about doing what you love and meeting people with similar interests, but it also can (and should!) make you a little money while you're at it. After all, if you want to do what you love, the model only works if it supports you in return. This is not to say that you should focus all your time and energy on making your blog profitable, but there are ways to monetize your blog that will not negate the enjoyment you get out of writing it.

One of the ways to monetize your blog is through sponsored posts. You will still get to write your own post, and write about what you love, but you get paid to do it. It is can be your first step into writing for profit, like a *real* author.

Getting your post sponsored is a very basic idea – you write about a product, website, or service that you love, and that company pays you for the free publicity. Obviously, if it were as easy as writing a few hundred words and then watching the cash flow in, everyone would be doing it. It's not quite that easy, but don't be scared away!

First of all, you probably want to announce at the beginning or the end of your blog (or in a pre-publication post) that you are doing a sponsored post, as people don't mind sponsorships as long as they're not deceived into reading something. Everyone understands that you need to pay the bills, but no one likes being tricked into reading an advertisement.

Second – all you have to do is ask! It really is that simple. Start with people and products that you really, truly believe in – that blog you love, that shampoo you can't get enough of, the website you're practically addicted to. Shoot off an e-mail or call the public relations department. The worst that can happen is they politely say no (very few professionals are going to yell at you for asking) or not answer at all. That's not very painful!

You might have to ask many, many times, but eventually you *will* find a sponsor. Then, just write the post! Be honest and enthusiastic. Your readers will really respond this this. Don't ask to be sponsored by someone you just want to bad-mouth. That kind of negativity just leads to bad karma. Remember the rule – if you wouldn't say it in front of your grandmother, don't say it on the internet. You wouldn't bad-mouth a stranger in front of grandma, would you?

Sponsored posts are a great way to make a little money, add variety to your blog, and support a cause you really believe in. They are definitely not something you want to do everyday, or every week, but they can be a great addition to your blog.

Tip from Jill -

You can be a sponsored blogger, just like athletes can be sponsored runners, swimmers, race car drivers, etc. The hardest part is asking!

Chapter 17- Social Media – An Introduction

Here is the secret of many bloggers – they started out in social media. This can seem like kind of a shameful admission, because it has shades of teenagers just trying to become celebrities on Twitter. But there is nothing to be ashamed of!

Social media has been one of the biggest revolutions in modern history. Almost everyone across the globe now has a "presence" online through Facebook, Twitter, Instagram, or any of the many regional variations. We are all connected with each other, in a way that other inventions like the telegraph or telephone never even approached. So why is it such a surprise that many bloggers started out posting their ideas and musings on social media, and then branched out into a format that didn't limit their thoughts to 140 characters?

Because there is a stigma attached to social media, many bloggers abandon their accounts and never look back. Others scale back to keep their blogs strictly professional (whatever that definition may be for the blog), and their social media accounts solely personal. The problem here is, though, that there is an untapped wealth of readers waiting to find you, and social media is the quickest and easiest way to reach them.

Bloggers need to start returning to social media. They don't have to completely mix their blog announcements and Facebook accounts, flooding their friends' News Feeds with blog posts and links, but they shouldn't pretend that one doesn't exist when they are on the other.

In the coming chapters, we are going to talk about the different social media sites, how to promote your blog on them without being obnoxious, and their different strengths and weaknesses. If you are already a blogger who wasn't afraid of their social media roots, I believe I can still give useful advice to you, too. There are many ways to promote yourself, and making use of all the best social media sites is very important.

Tip from Pinal -

Becoming a blogger does not mean that you can shut down your Facebook and Twitter account. On the contrary, make your social media websites work for you.

Chapter 18 - Facebook

For better or worse, Facebook is the leader of social media. When you say "social media" the blue "F" is what most people think of. It has over one BILLION users (that is 1/7th of the population of the earth). The average user scrolls through 1500 posts EVERY DAY, and spends about eight hours on the website every month. Many users access the site both on home computers and on mobile devices, and have nearly 24 hours of possible Facebook access.

In the sense of advertising a business, Facebook has huge potential – and businesses know this, based on the number of ads appearing the website. There are about 1 million advertisers on Facebook, and while exact numbers are not available, it is believed that Facebook charges about $2.5 million for the rights to post a video ad. If you want to reach people, Facebook is clearly the way to go.

So what is a little blog to do? Think about your own Facebook usage. How often do you check Facebook? How often do you click on the ads? What are you more likely to click on? I hope that you are reaching the same conclusions as me.

I want to emphasize that you do NOT have to have a large bankroll to make Facebook work for you and your blog. In fact, Facebook accounts for users are free, and bloggers should take advantage of this! You should be using your Facebook profile to advertise your blog.

Every time you post something new on your blog, update your Facebook status with the news, and a link to the blog (important). Every time you have a contest or giveaway, update Facebook. If you update your contact info, change your layout, or add information, update Facebook! You might feel a little shy about sharing this part of your life with your friends, but let me be the first to tell you – if they are true friends, they will WANT to hear about this part of your life. If you still feel uncomfortable, create another Facebook account (still free!) just for your blogging purposes, but be sure to reach out to readers and interested friends to grow your followers, don't wait for them to come to you (if you already have a profile, they may never find you).

I cannot emphasize enough that Facebook is an incredible tool that will help readers find you. If you are already a Facebook user, take a few minutes to share about your blog right now. Don't be shy. If you do not have an account, you should seriously consider creating one – it really is the current leader in social media. If you are still uncomfortable, please consider using one of the many other sites that we will be covering in the upcoming chapters.

Tip from Jill -

Love it or hate it, Facebook is the first site to look for when you want to start generating word-of-mouth buzz about your blog. If you're uncomfortable using your personal account, start a fan page for your site.

Chapter 19 - Google+

In the last chapter, we talked about the social media giant, Facebook. I hope you all read it and went away understanding how serious we think social media is for bloggers. Blogging is itself a form of social media, and very rarely do you get the chance to have crossover between the platforms (very few people post on Facebook "Hey, check out my Twitter!").

Right now, we're going to talk about Google's social media offering, Google+. It could jokingly be referred to as Facebook's little brother, but Google+ really has its own strengths and weaknesses, and just because you have Facebook doesn't mean you should overlook Google+.

To start out with, Google+ is a great alternative to Facebook if you are uncomfortable with its privacy policy, target audience (30% of users are 15-34), or just don't want to cave in and get a Facebook account since you've held out this long. There is still a large audience to reach on Google+ (including overlap from users who also have a Facebook account) – about 300 million users at last count.

Another perk of Google+ is that you can assign all your friends to different circles – so if you know your grandma won't care about your technical blog, you only need to share that information with your "Friends" circle instead of your "Family" circle (although, give your grandma a little credit, she might want to know all about your technical interests!). There is also the fact that many technically-minded people prefer Google+ to Facebook, so if you have a highly technical blog, this might be the social media site of your target audience.

My advice, for what to post on Facebook holds true for Google+, too. Whenever you have a new blog post, tell Google+. Contests and giveaways – put it on Google+. If you update your contact info, change your layout, or add information – put it on Google+. I think of it like the old adage – if a tree falls in the woods, and no one is around to hear it, does it make a noise? If you put something on your blog, but no one knows, is your blog truly successful?

I don't believe in defining myself as a blogger based on how many readers I have. I believe that if you are writing about something you love, and posting it in a public place, you are a blogger. But having readers is so fun! It is the true perk of blogging. They give you feedback, they create a community, and it is always great to talk to people who share your interests. Social media is one way to attract readers, and its power should not be overlooked.

Tip from Pinal -

Google+ is Facebooks biggest competition. Don't think of it as a one-or-the-other choice for yourself though, you definitely can use both social media sites for your blog.

Chapter 20 - LinkedIn

LinkedIn often gets overlooked in the social media website realm. It was created as a way for a business professional to connect to others in their field, and as such, it is not the kind of website that people surf daily. I am a big believer in LinkedIn (even, or maybe *especially*, for non-bloggers). It might not be the most fun social media websites, but connecting professionally is extremely important.

If you are completely unaware of LinkedIn, let me give you a little bit of background. You create a profile, much like any other social media platform, but instead of your interests, hobbies, and current employer, you also post all the information that is also on your resume. Then you start connecting to people you work with, businesses you'd like to worth with, and others who may be helpful or connected to your professionally. Co-workers can verify that you know the skills you list. A basic account is free, but if you pay for a Premium account, you can connect with potential employers or employees directly, and see who is viewing your profile (a great lead when searching for a new job).

So, right now, you might be asking yourself what use LinkedIn can be to you as a blogger. The answer is – if you want to be a professional blogger at all,

LinkedIn is very important! If you currently have a different "day job," you can still connect with people on LinkedIn who have more to do with the blogging world – in fact, since you spend most of your time at a different job, this might be the only way to socially connect with other bloggers or blogging resources.

If you have a technical blog at all, connecting with other professionals is very important. They can be a great resource for information for your blog, act as guest hosts or guest bloggers, and a really great way to find potential readers. Just like any other social media site, you can post information about your blog on LinkedIn, live.

At this point, I feel like I am just echoing myself, but it bears repeating: Every time you post something new on your blog, update LinkedIn (and add a link to the post). Every time you have a contest or giveaway, update LinkedIn. If you update your contact info, change your layout, or add information, update LinkedIn!

Tip from Jill -

LinkedIn is a social media website for professionals. If your blog is about professional or technical details – definitely use it to alert readers

about your blog. If you want to further your career as a blogger, definitely look into making a profile.

Chapter 21 - Twitter

When I include Twitter in social media lists, some readers get confused. Isn't Twitter a type of blog as well? The answer here is that it is both! Twitter really emphasizes how social media and blogging are intertwined and overlapping. When blogging or Tweeting, you are putting information out there for others to absorb, comment on, and share. It is BEING social. With that said, if you have a "full size" blog, don't overlook Twitter!

Twitter is probably the second largest social media website after Facebook. Numbers for the number two spot disagree, but Twitter *is* extremely popular, and I encourage using every social media website you can, so it doesn't matter who is number one, two, and three, you should be using all of them. From my point of view, there are many potential readers on Twitter, and not all of them have Facebook accounts, so if you really want to cover all your bases, get a Twitter account!

So what exactly *IS* Twitter? A "microblog" doesn't really explain very much. On Twitter, anyone with an account can post whatever is on their mind (up to 140 characters) and anyone can read it. Users can follow their favorites, so that when they log in to their accounts, tweets from their favorites are right there on their home page, easy to read and easy to access. You can post text, pictures, and links on Twitter (again, up to 140 characters).

Can you see how this can be an amazing tool for bloggers? You don't have to worry about taking up someone's time, or filling up their news feed with information they don't care about. Twitter is meant to collect little bits of a lot of information for easy access. You also know that if someone is following you, they WANT to see that information.

Twitter is also the true user of the "hashtag." Adding a "#" to keywords helps Twitter users search for and find content they care about. Shorted URLs are also important for Twitter – links can sometimes take up more than 140 characters, so using a URL shortener like goo.gl, bit.ly, or TinyURL, is important if you want readers to be able to click on links.

As with any social media website, I encourage you to post on Twitter every time you write a new blog, every contest, giveaway, and website update.   But because Twitter is a way to get little bits of information out there, you can post so much more!   Poll your readers for information, ask about current events, link to the blogs you're reading, I could extend this list almost infinitely. Twitter is a way to get your name out there, and KEEP it there.

Tip from Pinal -

Twitter is one of the easiest ways to start a social media presence. You don't even have to write a lot to get your profile out there – your limit is 140 characters.

Chapter 22 - Pinterest

If you are only passingly aware of Pinterest, the idea of it as a social media website might be something of a surprise to you.   It is kind of like an online scrapbook, where users can "pin" pictures they like onto "boards" (like pasting a picture onto a page), and give them themes. Many people use Pinterest to collect fashion and beauty ideas, decorating ideas, or just beautiful or interesting content they want to collect in one place.

This seems like a solo activity, but Pinterest is so much more! You can post your boards publicly, and other users can connect with you through them – creating a community of like-minded individuals. See? Anything can be social media when you get people connecting to each other!

So how can a blogger use Pinterest? If you are an artist-type blogger, Pintrest has endless possibilities. If you post artwork, photographs, poetry, collages, images of things you've made by hand, post them on Pinterest, too! Provide lots of links to your blog, and connect with the people who connect with you on Pintrest, letting them know your blog is a place to find more of the same.

More of a technical blogger, with less visual media to show others? Don't be afraid to share flow charts or diagrams – anything visual – on Pinterest. You never know who might be out there whose attention you might catch. Pinterest is also becoming a great site for humor. Many people surf Pinterest looking at funny sayings and pictures. Start pinning funny things front your field – you can even cross post your board to your blog. Humor is a great way to connect with people.

Whether or not you feel that Pinterest is a social media site that works for your blog, I hope you are coming away from this article with one thing in mind – connecting with readers and possible readers is an incredibly important part of blogging, and you should go to where the people are. Meet them on their own ground, and tell them what you have to offer. You might even be able to think of a site that wouldn't normally be considered "social media," but is a great way to connect with others.

Tip from Jill -

Pinterest seems more like an online bulletin board, but you can use it as social media to post images from your blog and get your name out there.

Chapter 23 - Tumblr

Let me be honest right from the very beginning – Tumblr can be a confusing place! It can be just about whatever the Tumblr user wants it to be – it can be a blogging platform for full sized blogs. It can be a place to repost things that they liked on the other (any) website. It can be photographs, original artwork, or artwork from somewhere else, altered and reposted.

There is no comment section on Tumblr, just a place to "like" a post or reblog it – and then that content goes to your own Tumblr page. It can be like reading a blog, reading a scrap book, or a completely nonsensical collection of photos, gifs, and text that only makes sense if you know the individual.

The creators of Tumblr market are a "the way blogging is supposed to be" - completely free form and a little anarchic. So is there a place for traditional bloggers looking for readers on Tumblr? I hope you know my answer is going to be – of course!

First off, Tumblr might just be a place you go to find interesting content that can give you ideas and let you know what is going on in your community. Some users have described Tumblr like falling down the rabbit hole in the book *Alice in Wonderland* – you stumble from one subject to another, and before you know it, it's midnight and you've wasted an entire day. While this can be entertaining and rewarding, lets not forget the "social connection" aspect.

Find the content you like, and "like" it officially. This gets your name out there, and if you create a Tumblr account, reblog it and you're attracting a new place for readers to find you and what you like! If this still seems a little scary, just stick to checking out Tumblr for ideas.

However, I think that from every scary situation, something can be learned (maybe that is part of what is scary – learning can be hard!). Tumblr might not be for everyone, but it is still a great place to meet people and learn things. As a social media website, it is certainly "up and coming," and shouldn't be overlooked.

Tip from Pinal -

Tumblr is in a class of its own. It might not be the easiest place to get your name "out there," but it is a great resource for bloggers nonetheless.

Chapter 24 - Gauging popularity With Klout

So we have learned about creating our own blog, choosing a platform, and writing content. We covered gaining readers through contests, giveaways, and promotions. We learned about using social media to get our names out there and to gain readership. But sometimes blogging can still feel like shouting into the dark. Is there anyone out there? Is anyone listening?

There are many ways to gauge how popular your blog is. Your blogging platform may even have built-in options to check how many visitors your blog is receiving – you can even put a counter on your page to show how many visitors it has received. If you're interested in this at all (or think you may be in the future) this is something to keep in mind when choosing a blogging platform. Almost all platforms will have this widget option.

Opening up a comment section can also be a way to gauge your popularity. Looking at the number of comments and commenters will quickly show you an estimate of your readers. Obviously there will always be "lurkers" – people who read but do not comment on your blog – but comments will at least show you how many active readers you have.

Checking your blog popularity can also be as simple (and free) as doing a Google search of your name or your blog's name. Where you pop up in the search results will quickly show you how well you are doing. A more stringent search – for your topic, rather than your name – will also show you how popular you are in your field.

But if you want an exact number, a tool that can show you how you're doing and what you can do to make it better, I suggest Klout. Klout is a website that uses a variety of parameters (like Google rankings, but also Wikipedia and a proprietary formula), and combines to give you a score out of 100. The higher your number, the more popular you are. It will also give you an idea of what you need to work on to start ranking higher.

Checking your popularity can be a loaded question – sort of like eavesdropping on a conversation about you. Do you really want to know what people *really* think? If your goal is to become a famous blogger, I highly encourage checking these stats. If you are an "every day" blogger and just creating a community, proceed with caution.

Tip from Jill -

When you were in high school, did you ever wish there was a computer program that could tell you how popular you were? Well, with Klout, your dreams have come true.

Chapter 25 - Design Elements – An Introduction

Having a well-designed blog is an important part of having a well-read blog. There are plenty of blogs out there that are boring, confusing, or (I'm sorry to say) just plain ugly. Some of these blogs are also popular – but let's face it, it can be very difficult to draw in readers with your content if your layout is driving them away. A well-designed blog is going to make your life easier.

The first step to creating a well-designed blog is to recognize the important parts of a blog. These parts are called "elements," and you will recognize them as soon as they are named.

Header: the headline or title at the top of your blog. It is usually the blog's name, icon, or a quotation that is pertinent to the blog.

Footer: this is the information at the bottom of a blog page. It is usually contact info, legal consideration, or the blog icon.

Side bar: this is a column running along the left or (usually) right side of a blog. It is usually static – meaning it doesn't scroll as you scroll down through the blog posts. It usually contains author information, archives, links to popular posts, and links to other blogs. This part is totally up to you!

Posts: yes, this is really the final piece of a blog – blogs are very simple! Your blog may have one post per page, or many posts – it is usually a good idea to limit the number to five to 10, though, as constant scrolling can get tiresome.

Extras – there are other things you can use to spruce up your blog.

Widgets/Apps: your blogging platform may provide all sorts of nifty tools you can pin to your blog – visitor counters, social networking links, e-mail links, countdown clocks, the list could go on! Use these sparingly so you don't overwhelm your content with widgets.

Ads: Ads are a way to monetize your blog, and if you're using Google's popular AdWords, you can control where they appear – in between posts, in a sidebar, top, bottom, or any combination of the above. As with widgets, use them sparingly or you'll clutter up your blog.

Calendar/Archive: this is usually contained in the sidebar, but depending on the style of your blog, you can put it wherever you want! The calendar can be in a regular calendar style, a list, or whatever you think will fit your blog best.

This is by no means a comprehensive list, but some of the main "building blocks" of what goes into a successful blog. If you have one, some, or all of these elements, you are on your way to building a great blog.

Tip from Pinal -

Readability is a very important part of a good blog. Designing your blog to be easy-to-read from the very start cannot be underestimated.

Chapter 26 - Choosing a Domain Name

Having a catchy title is important to a blog. If you have thought about having a blog, talked to someone, idly toyed with the idea one day – you have heard this advice. Hearing it repeated doesn't make it any easier to pick a good name for your blog – one that is memorable, catchy, on-topic, and if you're lucky, a little bit funny, too.

Unfortunately, I cannot help you choose a blog name – that hard work is up to you! But once you've chosen a name, deciding on a domain name is almost as important. The domain name is the web address, or URL, that people will use to find your blog. There are so many reasons that a good domain name is important, let me start with the most important (to my mind).

To me, being found by search engines is incredibly important. Your blog will get noticed through word of mouth, linking to other bloggers, becoming part of a community, but you cannot overlook having people find you through web searches – all part of SEO, Search Engine Optimization.

SEO means that you need to include some key words in your domain name. This means that funny blog names, or ones with puns in the title, might get overlooked by search engine. If your blog about eggs has the domain name www.theyolksonyou.com, search engines might not find your blog unless someone searches for "yolk."

I could go on and on about puny blog names, but the best advice I can give is: use common sense. When you choose a blog name, sleep on it, and if it seems like a silly idea in the morning, it's time to reconsider.

Other things to consider when choosing a domain name: spelling. If you are trying to make a plural or possessive name, make sure there aren't too many "s"s in a row, which can be difficult to read and type correctly.

When you are searching for a blog name, you might find that your name is already taken. Trying "unique" spellings of your name might also lead to confusion – you might be surprised how hard it is to purposely make a typo! Getting a name too close to an already-existing blog might just drive traffic to someone else's blog, not your own.

Keep it short. It might be tempting to make your domain name your entire blog name plus tag – ending up with a 30 or 40 character domain names. The difficulty in remembering and typing a name like this might actually lose readership – they might get bored and just leave before they finish typing! This is a sad but true fact.

These are only a few rules that you will hear about how to choose a domain name. You might be thinking that it is impossible to choose THE perfect blog name. And that is probably true. The best you can do is pick one that is good enough for your purposes, and one that you are happy with.

Tip from Jill -

Your URL is going to follow your blog around forever. Choosing the perfect one is no easy task. The best advice – use a strong keyword, and avoid misspellings

Chapter 27 - Color

You might be wondering right now – what can color possibly have to do with a blog? Unless your blog is about painting or coloring books, it seems like a non-issue. And if we're talking about style, it's not like painting a room – it is the internet! If you're unhappy with it, change it! And for the most part, you are right. Changing the color of a blog is very easy, depending on your blog platform, but keeping readers happy with blog colors is kind of tricky.

It is true – the color of your blog, specifically the background and text color, is going to determine the mood of your readers. There is scientific evidence that color affects mood. And to make things even more tricky, colors have different meaning in different cultures.

For example, in some cultures, red is associated with heat, anger, and fire. Other cultures associate red with mourning, other with happiness. From individual to individual, it might bring pleasant memories, or be their least favorite color. Others might just think of ketchup.

Scientifically, green is supposed to be the most soothing and calming color, probably because of its connection to nature. But some cultures use green as a color mourning, and many others think of it as the color of money (which is not necessarily a calming thought!).

There is no reason to be paralyzed by the fear of using color on your blog, but you should definitely get a few opinions before you settle on one color scheme. Also keep in mind that once you choose a color, *technically* you can just switch it if you don't like it. But switching colors on a blog can be confusing to readers – especially if you abruptly change color schemes after a very long time, or go through a period of lots of color changing.

No matter what color you ultimately choose, consistency is probably what most readers are looking for. While the world of blogging is sort of "fast and loose," readers still crave consistency. Imagine yourself in the readers spot. You log on to your favorite blog, expecting something familiar and comforting, with new information to digest. But you are greeted with a flashy new background. The layout is all different. Where is the new post? You can't navigate! You're confused!

Color and consistency go hand-in-hand. Whatever you choose, be happy enough to stick with it for the foreseeable future. Your readers will not only thank you – they will show their gratitude by coming back over and over, and becoming regular readers (the best kind of reader a blogger could ask for).

There is also readability to consider. Black text on a white background might scream "boring!" to more artistic types, but it is definitely the easiest color combination to read on a computer screen. Even a dark background with light text can be difficult to decipher depending on screen size, room brightness, and resolution of the monitor. And don't forget that more and more people are accessing the internet on smart phones now. Imagine how hard it would be to read a blog on a smart phone with black background and neon green text!

The use of color (or no color) on your blog is going to be a personal choice, and there is no right or wrong answer. The best advice I can give is to have multiple people take a look at your blog online and on paper, and give you their honest opinions.

Tip from Pinal -

There is not one color that I can say is the perfect one for every blog. Choose one for good readability. White is always easy on the eyes.

Chapter 28 - Photos

Do I really need to start this chapter out with "A picture is worth 1,000 words"? Do I need to tell you that in our modern age, pictures are what capture the attention? I'm sure everyone here has not only heard this a million times, but has noticed it themselves, as they cruise the internet and skip over what looks like giant chunks of text with no photos.

So let's just agree, pictures are really important. You don't need to have a photojournalism blog to know that you should have a few photos on your blog, if not a small one to introduce every post. This is something to consider when choosing a blog platform, right at the very beginning – how many photos can you post, and how easy is it to do with this platform (the range goes from a piece of cake to infuriatingly complicated).

So let's say you have a technical blog – should you still include photos? I'm sure you are nodding along to this answer already – ABSOLUTELY! Even very technical blogs should include illustrations (screen shots) of more complicated issues. Remember, not everyone who reads the blog is going to be an expert – they might be trying to learn as well.

Pictures can also be used to lighten the mood. There are many stock photos of people making funny faces, or the ubiquitous "cats in funny poses" that, thrown into a blog, can add some humor to a very dry subject. Some blogs will even allow you to insert charts, graphs, and other informative images. You can find these images in any price range – very high (for high quality), to a few dollars, to free.

There are many ways to use pictures, as well. Sometimes I think that the hallmark of an amateur blogger is one who posts one giant or one tiny photo at the beginning of their blog post, and it is the only photo on the whole page. Once you become more comfortable with blogging and more familiar with what your blog platform is capable of, you will soon find many ways to use images.

First – right at the top. Amateurs gravitate there for a reason! You can place a large, eye-catching photo right here, for maximum impact. Next: sides. Think of how newspaper columns are laid out. You can place an image on the far left or right and format your text around it. This can be good to break up large chunks of text, and also to highlight important points.

Last: not in your post at all! Don't forget that the posts on your page will change almost every day (depending on how often you post). Include an author photo, or avatar if a photo of you in public makes you uncomfortable – readers will have a face to put with the voice. Blogging is a community, and it is hard to feel connected to an anonymous author.

Use a nice image as the banner for your blog. Think of it like a welcome mat for your readers – something they'll come to recognize as a signpost for good content. If you feel really artistic, design a logo for your blog – one that will go in the header, act as an avatar on social media sites, and become your trademark.

Images of all kinds have a place on your blog, and are an integral part that should not be overlooked.

Tip from Jill -

Wherever and whenever possible, use pictures on your blog. They break up large chunks of text, and draw the reader's eye.

Chapter 29 - Adding Extra Pages

Blogs are a strange hybrid of a static website and a constantly changing social media website. The content constantly changes, but can be easily accessed. There are static features as well as constantly changing things. Blogs are often compared to newspapers or websites, because the content is updated.

Dedicated newspaper or magazine subscribers, though, will say that these print items are also familiar and comforting, because there are constants – the banner headline, the writers, the different but consistent sections (news, arts, fashion, comics, etc). This is something that blogs can learn from print media – consistency.

People are creatures of habit and will be searching for the familiar, even while they are searching for new content on your blog. So how can you incorporate that on your blog, when you are constantly updating with new posts?

The answer is in the "extra" pages. The number and kind may be dictated by your blog platform, but many of them allow any number – so feel free to use any or all of these ideas. The most common extra is "about me." It might just be one paragraph in the far right column of your blog, with a small avatar and two sentences about you and your interest. It can be this same information, but on its own page (with a link on the main page, of course!). You can write as much or as little about yourself as you want. Readers will be curious about you, though – they want to put a face to the voice – so try to include a little bit.

You can also include contact information – on its own page, or in the "about me" section. If you have a highly technical blog, you may want to include a blog-specific e-mail address for inevitable questions. If you have co-authors or regular contributors, they can provide contact information here, too, in case there are questions you can't answer.

Some blogs are now including links to their own favorite blogs or resources. Readers may like this option, as it will give them more reading material and can help them delve deeper into a subject they are really interested in or are just starting to learn about. Outside resources can be included as links in the far right column or on a page of their own.

Extra pages can be as numerous and varied as your imagination. These are just simple guidelines to get you thinking about what might be useful to have on your own blog.

Tip from Pinal -

Readers are going to be curious about you. An "About Me" page, "Contact Me," "Additional Info" page is going to make you more accessible and keep readers happy.

Chapter 30 - To Comment or Not to Comment

Comments on blogs are a great way to interact with your readers, to hear what they have to say about what you have written, and to see how they interact with each other in discussions of your work. They can be an amazing place to learn, make friends, and grow in your chosen blogging field.

But they can also be minefields of hurtful comments, unnecessary information, and spamming. Comments on a blog are a double-edged sword – while there are many benefits, there are also many drawbacks, enough to scare some bloggers away from comments altogether.

I think that disabling comments on your blog is a very sad situation. It is very easy to become a "loner" on the internet – finding the information you care about, without sharing it with anyone around you (in cyberspace or real life). Think about the stereotype of someone sitting in the dark, hunched over a glowing computer screen, alone in their thought and alone in the world.

Comments on a blog (or any website) can erase this image. You can interact with real people, in real time, and discuss topics you love. They may be thousands of miles away, or right down the street – but it is still a set of people who you might never interact with in real life. This is the beauty of the internet age – I believe that technology can bring us together, it isn't only driving us apart as some people fear.

Now that you know my glowing recommendation for comments on a blog, let me address the darker side of the comments section. If the blogger is not vigilant, the comment section can quickly become a haven for spammers and trolls. Spammers will post the same thing about making "thousands of dollars in a day!" and "cheap drugs available online!" over and over and over… effectively shutting down the comment section of a blog.

Trolls are a worse breed, who post hateful, inflammatory comments just to start fights and upset people. It is like yelling something nasty out of a car window, and then driving away. Because there is nothing obviously suspicious about their accounts (they are posting original content every time, and don't have an obvious fake name), they can be very tricky to screen out even with the best monitoring software.

There are definitely ways to outsmart the spammers and trolls. There are many commenting software programs that help you screen out the spammers (the same way your spam filter works on your e-mail) and depending on your blog platform, you can use commenting applications that require users to create a permanent account – the loss of anonymity cuts down on trolling.

If all else fails, you can opt to screen every post that appears on your blog. On a popular blog or a popular individual post, this can be extremely time consuming – but definitely a way to ensure that only the high quality comments appear.

I am still a big believer in the community a comments section can create on a blog. My advice to new bloggers is to enable comments, but to keep a close eye on it to weed out spammers and trolls. If you are diligent, many spammers and trolls will come to recognize that your blog is not going to allow them to run the comment section.

Tip from Jill -

Comments are both the lifeblood and the bane of a blog. They can foster great discussions, and become a cess pit of trolling and name-calling. I encourage comments for all blogs – but I also encourage patrolling them closely.

Chapter 31 - Ethics & Legal Issues

Blogging is still a very new technology – and it is changing so fast that local and international laws are having a hard time keeping up. Some bloggers think this means they can live above the law, and can post anything they'd like without repercussions. Please do not do this! This is the sign of a lazy, poor quality blog.

With that said, there are a few ethical and legal issues that all bloggers should look out for – don't worry, this isn't going to be full of legal jargon, the rules are actually quite simple. There is basically one rule: no stealing.

This doesn't mean "don't steal candy bars from the other blog" – except in a way, it does. Let me explain – don't steal content from other blogs. Don't steal content from *someone* – websites, books, movies. Whether they are popular or completely unknown – it is still known as plagiarism. This one of the biggest ethical issues for blogs. It can seem so innocent at first – maybe you meant to quote your favorite book, but forgot to use quotation marks. Maybe you found an obscure blog you love, and it seems so simple just to copy and paste on that day you have writer's block. Plagiarism is the number one way blogs lose credibility, respect, and readers.

Related to plagiarism is copyright or trademark infringement. It is also stealing – but usually of images or trademarked logos rather than text. The best way to avoid this is to use, reliable stock photo websites when you need something for your blog.

Those are the main legal issues you may encounter as a blogger. There are other ethical issues to keep in mind – ones that are not typically illegal, but are a matter of politeness and courtesy. As in life – the best rule of thumb is to keep things polite. It may be extremely tempting to use your blog as a soap box for airing your personal grievances – with other bloggers, with people in your life, companies, the list could go on and on – but these things are probably best left unsaid.

My favorite rule of thumb for these situations is – would you say this in front of your grandparents? Think of a person in your life who believes in the best parts of you, and who you would do anything to live up to these expectations – usually a grandparent figure. You wouldn't want to be caught by a grandparent saying hurtful things about someone – so don't post them on your blog.

Beyond these rules – your blog is your blank canvas. It is your place to learn, to teach, and to form a community. The world of blogging is still constantly changing and can seem frightening to jump into. I hope this blog chapter has made the pressing legal issues more clearly, so that new bloggers have one less thing to worry about as they jump into this exciting new world.

Tip from Pinal -

The world of blogging can be a little bit like the Wild West. Just because there are few rules, that doesn't mean plagiarism, stealing, and copyright infringement is OK on your blog.

Chapter 32 - Blog Etiquette

In the last chapter in this book, we talked about legal and ethical issues surrounding blogging. In it, we mentioned my favorite rule of thumb: if you wouldn't say it in front of your grandparents, don't put it on your blog. It is part of my ethical "code of conduct." I think that this rule of thumb can also be used as an etiquette guide as well.

Etiquette is a strange area, where it seems pointless in our new, technological world. Some people hear the word "etiquette" and have immediate mental images of ladies wearing gloves and hats at all times, drawing rooms, tea parties, and thick etiquette manuals full of conflicting advice.

To me, though, etiquette has a definite place in the modern world – perhaps now more than ever. We are becoming more and more interconnected through the whole world, where language barriers and cultural differences divide us at the same time as common interests unite us. This can lead to a world full of missteps and sensitive areas.

What is the best way to deal with this – etiquette! I don't mean long lists of which spoon to use and what colors are appropriate to wear. To me, etiquette is another word for – be polite. Treat others as you would like to be treated. Think before you speak (or type).

These are simple rules that we learn as children. However, in the new world on the internet, these rules can seem unimportant or are totally forgotten – why bother people polite to a person half a world away, whose face, as far as you know, is a simple gray outline. Why not say something hurtful, knowing that you will never see them or their avatar again – in the real world or on the internet.

This kind of attitude, though, is what scares people away from blogging, blogs, and participating in comment sections. If we all followed and promoted the simple rules of politeness, the internet would be a better place to be.

On top of this, following these rules as a blogger will give your blog an aura of respectability. If you are known as the blogger who doesn't attack others, it can lead to more business and contacts. You can build up a community of individuals with similar interest and goals. In the blogging business, this is solid gold. It can lead to more readers, more advertisement guest posts and guest posters. Your blog is an individual effort, but it doesn't have to stay that way forever.

Maybe my ideas about etiquette and politeness are old-fashioned, but I truly believe that a little bit of kindness will go a long way in this business that is basically a frontier. We are truly making the rules as we go along – let's make them the *right* rules.

Tip from Jill -

A good reputation is worth holding on to. Following good etiquette rules will mark you as a quality blogger.

Chapter 33 - Comment Etiquette

We have been talking a lot the last few chapters about ethical and etiquette issues. If you have been paying attention, you know that I am a big believer in politeness and treating others with kindness. So, if you disagreed with any of those sentiments, you are not going to enjoy what I have to say about comment etiquette.

We have also discussed the wild world that is blog comment sections. They can be a great place to form a community for your blog, but if you are not careful, it can also devolve into a frightening arena of hateful comments and spam. If any place can use some etiquette rules, it is the comment section!

There are two aspects to this problem – the commenter and the moderator (or blogger). As a commenter, follow the golden rule – do unto others as you would them do to you. Things to avoid: trolling, flaming, personal attacks… let me stop this list now! Sometimes in the course of comments you may say things you'd like to take back, but as in real life, we all make mistakes and as long as you are generally trying to be a good commenter, don't get scared away from your favorite blog comment sections.

As the person running a blog, you may decide to moderate your comments, that is, read all of them before they are allowed to appear on your blog. This is the best way to keep out spammers and trolls. Spam is very obvious and deserves to be immediately dismissed. Trolling, however, is a trickier etiquette subject.

Trolling, if you are not familiar with the term, is making a rude, inappropriate, off-topic, or simply mean comments, just to cause a fight or hurt feelings on a blog. Many are very obvious, and deserve to be dismissed out of hand. However, when you're typing on the internet, without facial cues and voice cues, your intent can be lost. A poorly phrased question can come out as inflammatory, or a legitimate misunderstanding can sound like rudeness.

When moderating comments, try to be impartial and allow ALL points of view to have their time, even if you don't agree with what they are saying. There is no easy way to make this call. We are all inherently biased creatures, with feelings that can be hurt and emotions that can be confused. The general rule is to dismiss obvious trolls and spammers, and to let nature take its course.

This can be a difficult task, especially with personal attacks, so try your best. If I had to make a pros & cons list about blogging, my pros list would be miles long, but dealing with trolling and spammers would probably be the only con. It is definitely a difficult subject, but I think that the joys of blogging and creating a community on a subject you love far outweigh any unpleasantness.

Tip from Pinal -

As a commenter, be polite and always reread what you're written before you hit "send." As a moderator, try to be tough but fair.

Chapter 34 - Blog SEO – An Introduction

SEO stands for Search Engine Optimization. It is a very hot topic right now – not only for bloggers, I bet that almost anyone who has read something on the internet has probably heard the term. The acronym is pretty self-explanatory – it is just a way to make your web site (or blog) more noticeable to search engines, right?

This is sort of like saying turning the key in the ignition is what makes the car go. It is technically true, but there are so many steps missing in between! Let us start at the very beginning. Search Engine Optimization means catching the attention of search engines, like Google, Yahoo, Bing, etc. But these search engines are not living beings, how do you capture a machine's attention?

Each search engine has its own algorithm, but they all send out bits of code or programming called "spiders," that literally crawl the internet (like a spider!) looking at the content of websites and logging it away to be catalogued and provided to users doing web searches. So, when we talk about SEO, we should be thinking of it as Search Engine Spider Optimization.

So what exactly is it that the spiders are looking for? One of the biggest things is keywords. Spiders are not sentient creatures, either, and they are basically doing word counts of the content of each page they find, and determine the subject matter of the page based on what words and phrases appear most often. That is why keyword density is important to SEO – if you are blogging about cupcakes, but you call them "tasty treats," "tiny delicacies," "everyone's favorite," instead of "cupcakes," the search engine spiders are not going to put your webpage very high in search results!

There is also no reason to repeat "cupcakes" over and over on a page just to get to be #1 on Google – search spiders are programmed to be smarter than that. A keyword density of 1-3% is best. There are other places to put keywords, too, that help search engine spiders categorize you. The ALT text on a photo or banner counts as a keyword (so that when a mouse hovers over that picture of a cupcake, the text that pops up says "cupcake"). It is also good to give your webpage a keyword as a web address. Cupcakes.com is probably no longer available, but delicious-cupcake-recipes.com may be available!

Search engine spiders have to search the *entire* internet, remember, so do not panic if your website or blog doesn't appear on Google for a few weeks (or even months, depending on how many visitors you get, word of mouth, etc.). You can submit your webpage to search engines to be indexed (the process is a bit different for each search engine), but this is not a guarantee that you will show up on page #1.

If you want to become really popular, you are going to have to rely on others. Blogs with more visitors are ranked higher by the search engine spiders. If your blog has lots of links leading to it, and lots of (good) links leading off of it, it is proof to the spiders that you are legitimate.

Becoming a Google star is hard work – and a path to follow. It probably will not happen to your site overnight, but if it is your goal, keep working at it and do the best job you can do. Quality will attract readership.

Tip from Jill -

As easy as it would be to ignore SEO and hope that it takes care of itself, it is an important skill for bloggers to learn. Despite the technical terms and "spiders," it is really not too difficult.

Chapter 35 - Off-Site Techniques

In the last chapter, we started talking about Search Engine Optimization (SEO). As you read it, you probably came away with the impression that keywords are the #1 way to attract search engine spiders to your site. Well, this is true, but it is not the *whole* truth. Keywords are going to take you a long way towards your goal, and they are important to keep in mind while you're building your website and during each post that you write. But there are other ways to attract search engine spiders that you can work on while you're not actively blogging.

In this chapter, we will talk about "off-site" or "off page" techniques. This is exactly what it sounds like – ways to get your blog's name out there, on pages other than your own. Renting an airplane to fly around a banner that says "READ MY BLOG" is one way to think of this, but in a virtual sense (don't rent a real airplane unless you are trying to target a very specific type of audience!).

Off-site techniques are really just links to your blog on other, reputable websites. It is a way for search engine spiders to check your references, in a way, to ensure that you are a legitimate blog and not just another spammer putting up a junk website to try to sell something or create ad revenue through clicks.

There once was a booming business of ways to buy off-site links, to make your blog appear very popular. However, search engines have really cracked down on this practice and have ways of detecting purchased links. Do not try this! It is a way to get yourself blacklisted by the spiders, and working your way back into their good graces will take a lot of time and hard work.

So, you are going to have to generate off-site links the old fashioned way, with good old networking. Having links to your blog on another related blog is the #1 off-site link. You can wait for people to find you and link to your material, or you can politely go around introducing yourself to the blogging community and asking for links – in return for linking to them, of course!

You can pay to advertise your blog on other blogs and websites. This is not the same as purchasing links, and should not hurt your optimization. News articles and press releases about your blog are also a great idea – and if you are not CNN level, ask friends to post press release style articles on their own websites. There are also websites that charge fees to post press releases about new blogs. Don't think of these as buying readership – many people actually browse these kinds of sites looking for new reading material. They have to find you somehow!

Also make sure your blog has a social media presence. Facebook is a way to get your friends to your blog, if you think they might be interested. You can also create a fan page for your blog on Facebook, as a way to help readers keep track of developments on your blog (90% of people will visit Facebook every day, so if you are there reminding them, they'll remember to visit your blog). You can also create a Twitter account for your blog, to keep readers up to date with new articles or features.

These are just a few off-site techniques you can try. These seem to be the tried-and-true methods. If you can think of other ways to market yourself and your blog, please feel free to give them a try!

Tip from Pinal -

You don't have to rely on your blog alone to bump your SEO rating. Try getting your name out there, on other blogs or websites, too.

Chapter 36 - On-Site Techniques

On-site Search Engine Optimization is the nuts and bolts of making a blog that is attractive to search engine spiders. It is not a secret code that will magically make your blog extremely popular overnight. These are tips and tricks to make your blog the best it can be, that will help you come to the attention of search engine spiders, and hopefully good search results will bring you readers – who are the true mark of blog popularity.

Here are some quick guidelines to SEO. It would be very easy to make this into a checklist, but I don't want to, you think of these as hard-and-fast rules. Some of these ideas will not work for your blog's style, format, or your manner of writing. These are just suggestions that have been proven to work that you should try.

First, certain kinds of content are attractive to search engine spiders. Posts that are about 500 words long, and are completely original – if you copy and paste from another source, spiders will pass right by your site! (Quoting is allowed, and yes, spiders can tell the difference between a short quote and a huge chunk of copied text.) Grammar and spelling mistakes will actually make your site less attractive to spiders, so be sure to use spell check!

Think of one or two keywords or phrases, and try to repeat them in your article for a keyword density of 1-3%. This is about three to ten uses of the word or phrase. If, when you read the post back to yourself, it sounds clunky and repetitive, you are over-using the word or phrase. Yes, it is that easy! Try to include the keyword or phrase in your title and in the link for the post, too.

There are other small ways to use keywords. If there are images linked with your post, you can create alt text, which is just a text ID for the image. Using a keyword as your ALT text is a good way to get spiders to notice you. Meta tags are similar, but for your post content. Meta tags are limited to about 160 characters, so be sure your keyword or phrase is some of them!

Link to other, legitimate websites in your post when necessary. These kind of links shows that you are a real website, not machine generated content, and will also give your readers more information. Search engine spiders do check out the links on your page, so make sure you're choosing wisely, and don't go overboard – the rule of thumb is that more than 100 links are a red flag to search engine spiders.

Above all, the best kind of Search Engine Optimization is good content. I cannot emphasize this enough. If you are writing the best posts you can, and truly trying to create a community of like-minded individuals, your readers will come. These tips and tricks are meant to speed your rise through the ranks – to keep you from slaving away in obscurity, creating amazing content that no one is reading. Having an active readership that leaves comments, uses your social media presence, and recommends you to others – that is when your blog truly becomes popular, no matter where Google or Yahoo say you rank.

Tip from Jill –

SEO is about more than the right keyword density and off-site techniques. To look legitimate to search engine spiders, it is important to have good links on your blog, too (even to other websites!).

Chapter 37 - Keywords, Metatags and Robots

A few chapters ago we talked about search engine spiders. Think of them like "code robots," that crawl around the internet, indexing everything they find. "Indexing" is also another term that you can guess the definition based on what it sounds like. When I think of indexing, I picture the 3"x6" cards that students use to make flash cards. Search engine spiders do something similar. Indexing is essentially making flash cards of the internet, making maps of what is where.

We have referred to the internet as the "World Wide Web" for so long, that people may actually picture a tangled web when they think of the internet. Even internet "addresses" give the idea that the internet is a physical space that needs mapping by search engine spiders.

Of course, this isn't called the "Digital Age" for nothing, the spiders are certainly not indexing actual, physical addresses. They are actually making notes of the keywords they find. "Aha!" you might be thinking, "keywords – this is a term that I know." Congratulations! And I hope that you are also using this term you know on your blog!

Search engine spiders make a note (and count!) the keywords on your blog, and use this to determine its topic, relevancy to web searches, and authenticity (making sure that you are not a robot, too). I hope that this has impressed on you the importance of keywords.

Another think spiders are indexing are the meta-tags. We have mentioned these before as well. Meta-tags are a few keywords that you can attach to images on your site. You will know them as the little boxes of text that pop up when you hover over an image on a website. These are meant to be notes to yourself, to remember what the picture is, but they have become increasingly important to SEO, once it was discovered that spiders are paying attention to them.

There are, of course, hundreds of little ways to capture the attention of search engine spiders, or to have your blog indexed by a search engine in other ways. However, these are the sure fire ways to be found, and also happen to be the easiest and most important (without them, you still may not be found, depending on what other pathways you take).

Tip from Pinal -

SEO is a simple concept, but difficult to execute. Just remember the big three: keywords, metatags and keeping the search engine spiders happy!

Chapter 38 - SEO-Friendly Site Design

At the word "design," some potential bloggers might be grimacing and about to leave to read Google News, or find more picture of kittens and puppies. Please stay with me! I promise this isn't going to be painful for all those non-artistic types.

Chances are, you have already put some thought into your blog design. If you have gone to a website and thought "yuck, this is hard to read," you already have some good tips and tricks under your belt! Trust me, you don't have to be a graphic designer to think about blog design.

If you already have a blog, and you already have put a title at the top, and picked a URL address close to the name of the blog, you have taken the most important steps towards good SEO friendly blog design. Think of design in this context as "easy to read" and "easy for search engine spiders to find."

We have already mentioned blog title and URL addresses. Please try to keep this as "on topic" as possible. It might be tempting to come up with a funny or "punny" name, but keep in mind that it will make it harder for people to find you. If you're willing to overcome this, or you are dedicated to getting your blog "out there" in other ways, or it is too late and you are locked into a name already, please just stay aware that there is extra work ahead of you.

Add a "keyword bank" to the end of your blog posts, or if your blogging platform allows, choose tags or categories to add to the post. A keyword bank is just a quick list of keywords that you feel sum up the post – 10-20 words will do. Tags or categories play the same role, but if you run a highly topical blog, will also save you some time by allowing you to click and choose, rather than having to think up 10 or 20 words for every single post. Tags and categories also make it easier for regular readers to find their favorite topics, because they are usually hyperlinked and can lead to as many related blog posts as you'd wish.

The whole point of this is to make sure that someone searching for that topic or keyword is more likely to find your website through Google, Yahoo, etc.

Honestly, we could talk for hours and hours about keyword density, posts per page, extra pages, off-site and on-site links – but these are really the main things to keep in mind. If you just want to write a few posts, stick them on your blog, and live the rest of your life not worrying about your blog – it really is this easy!

Tip from Jill -

Making your site design easy for SEO will make the rest of your job much easier. Pick the right URL, tag your posts, and use a keyword bank.

Chapter 39 - Search Engine Submission

We have talked a lot lately about search engine spiders. It is a very passive situation. You are essentially writing blog posts to an invisible audience, posting it on the internet, and hoping someone will stumble across you and love it, thereby vaulting you into fame and fortune. But what if you aren't really the "wait and see" type?

You can also go out and put your blog on a search engine yourself. This is called search engine submission, and as you might gather, it is going to be different for every different search engine, and may add up to a lot of work.

Search engine spiders often overlap, and while it make take a few weeks or months for them to find your blog, once you do it is almost like a party – more will start appearing. Once you are indexed, it will seem like they all have found you.

Search engine submission is the exact opposite. You have to go to each search engine yourself, and submit a form that details your website so that it can be manually indexed. The process is different for each site and can be somewhat confusing – probably to keep unscrupulous individuals from flooding the internet with sub-par material.

Here is the basic thing you have to do for search engine submission: some sites allow submitting one page at a time (or even prefer it). If you already have a huge blog with many pages, this can be a bit unwieldy. Other sites may only require submission of your home page, which is easier.

Other sites may require submission of a site map, which is a full run-down of your blog, with all the extra (about me, contact me, interesting stuff) links included. This is obviously a bit more complicated, especially if you don't already have one made (and sometimes they are made as a special page on your blog itself). Search engines may require one type of site map over another, so be sure to pay attention to the instructions.

When you are submitting your site, make sure you are ready. The quality of your blog is going to determine your page ranking – whether it shows up on page 1 or 100 on the search engine results. If you are a brand new blogger, aiming for page 1 is probably not realistic. But you also don't have to worry that there is going to be an individual pouring over your blog with a fine-tooth comb, looking for grammatical errors and poorly crafted sentences. They are just trying to confirm that you are not a spam-bot.

You just have to make sure that you are working links, a few posts, and are clearly an active poster (no changes in 6 months? Try updating regularly for a few weeks and then reconsider submitting).

Search engine submission is not a golden ticket to instant internet fame, but it is definitely a route to take to make sure you can be found.

Tip from Pinal -

Tired of waiting for search engine spiders to find you? You can always submit your site to the search engine databases yourself. It's not a sure-fire method, but it is better than languishing in obscurity.

Chapter 40 - Monetizing Your Blog

If you have accessed the internet at all in the past decade, you are aware that people can make money on blogs. This might seem like a crazy dream, like all the ads you see about miraculous weight loss and buying a home for only $1. The idea of becoming an internet billionaire might be a little far-fetched, but you *can* make money from blogging.

There are many, many ways to monetize your blog. It can be anything from allowing advertisements from outside sources, to selling times on your own blog. If your original intention was to sell your own items/services online, you still can consider a blog on top of an online store. Individuals are now visiting blogs, even for products they are interested in buying, as a way to get a feel for the company and the quality of product they might be investing in.

One of the most common ways to monetize a blog, though, is through advertisements. We will go deeper into this topic later, and even a full blog book will not be able to cover all the in-and-outs of advertising on a blog. However, most blog platforms have a built-in "allow advertising" option, and people are so used to ads on blogs that this might be the most unobtrusive way to try to make a little money.

There are different ways to make money off these ads, either by allowing a certain number, certain company, or time limit to ads. The most common is "pay per click," which gives you a few pennies every time someone clicks on an ad. This is also usually an option to choose on the dashboard of your blogging platform.

Instead of ads, you can also sell actual products on your blog. The most common is your blog-related items – like shirts and mugs (the most popular items anywhere). You can also sell items from a related blog or website (for a small fee on your part). Your whole blog can be dedicated to selling your own handcrafted item, with blog posts detailing every step of you making said item (hey, blog about whatever you'd like!).

Like a race car driver or professional athlete, you can also get sponsorships for your blog. This means that a company pays you to say "hey, this product is great!" because they think that your readers will go out and buy the product. This is obviously the realm of popular blogs with lots of readers, but it is definitely something to keep in mind as you learn and grow.

Some very lucky bloggers are going to be able to quit their day jobs and retire off the income from their blogs. If this is your goal, I encourage you to go for it! However, if you just like blogging and think it would be neat to make a little bit of "fun" money, monetizing your blog might be the pathway to a little extra income.

Tip from Jill -

Blogging for money might seem like a dream, but it is one that is attainable. There are many different ways, which we will cover in the next chapters.

Chapter 41 - AdSense

If you want to monetize your blog, you probably should start with Adsense. This is the premier way to put advertisements on your blog. It is the program that your blogging platform probably uses, and it is more user friendly than other options out there.

However, AdSense is not without its drawbacks. I don't want anyone to go into this thinking that AdSense is a miracle product. First of all – it puts ads on your blogs. Sometimes a distracting amount of ads that your readers will not like. And you don't get to choose which products are advertised.

Before you run away screaming, keep this in mind – AdSense *does* allow you to control the number and placement of ads, so you won't go from zero ads to "I can't find the blog post I'm trying to read" overnight. You can tell it whether to only allow side bar ads, or the middle of the page ads, or banner ads. AdSense does not allow pop-up ads.

AdSense is usually based on a "pay per click" model, which means that you get a few pennies every time someone clicks on one of the ads. Because very, very few people ever click on those "lose belly fat fast!" ads, AdSense usually tailors the advertisements to the topics of your blog.

This tailoring is made possible by the fact that search engine giant Google runs AdSense. They will use the same technology that puts the tailored ads next to your Gmail e-mails on your blog. Yes, it can be a little disconcerting (some people would say "creepy") but it is a technique that Google has proven to work.

Because AdSense is built in to blogging platforms – especially Google's platform, Blogger – is will be very easy to install on your blog.   It's not even an "installation" like you traditionally think about software. It really is logging in to your dashboard and putting some "yes" check marks in some boxes. Almost immediately, ads will appear on your blog.

If you are an established blogger with a dedicated readership, bear in mind that suddenly allowing ads on your blog might turn away some readers, who may think of you as a "sell out."   If you have a good relationship with your readers, most will stick it out, and you can even introduce the idea through blog posts, so there isn't an overnight change.   For established bloggers, some of the other monetizing options we will talk about might be better.

If you're a brand-new blogger, though, allowing a few (small!) ads on your blog from the very beginning is not a bad idea. It will not earn you a lot (or any) money at first, but you have set the standard for the future.   When you are an incredibly popular blogger with innumerable readers, they will not only be used to the idea of ads on your blog, but you have the opportunity to make quite a bit more money.

Tip from Pinal -

Adsense should be the first thing you try on your own blog. It is designed to be easy to use, and while it won't make you a millionaire, it is still a good tool.

Chapter 42 - Sponsorships

When I think about sponsorships, I think about the garish advertisements that are stuck to every square inch of racecars, or to every square inch of athletes. Brand names stuck to everything, from bumpers to running shoes. Honestly, I sometimes wonder if there is such an overload that they are completely ineffective anymore.

So why am I supporting such a useless, ugly waste on blogs? Well, for one thing, it is almost impossible to paste bumper stickers all over a blog. In the second place, many bloggers still want to actually blog, and no matter how many side bar, banner, and mid-page ads there are, the post is still prime. And in the third place, blog sponsorship is completely different than racecar or athletic sponsorship.

The basics are still going to be the same. A sponsor will find you (you are allowed to contact companies, too, more on that in a bit) and ask you to say nice things about them, in exchange for money. Sometimes this will be in the form of a larger-than-normal advertisement, or a whole post about the company/product. There is no set of rules about sponsorships (check with your blog platform first!) so the style can usually be negotiated with the sponsor.

You also don't have to sit around and wait to be asked.   If there is a company/product that you are super excited about, reach out to them with an offer. Be professional (of course) and as specific as possible – what you're willing to offer, how you envision the sponsorship appearing, what they will get out of it (how many readers you have, how much revenue you think it will generate) and a range that you'd like to be compensated.   Larger companies probably have a whole department devoted to screening these requests. The worst they can say is no!

Sponsorships do not mean that you have "sold out" the integrity of your blog. It means that you have reached a level of popularity that others deem you to have influence. With that said, it is usually courteous to alert readers that sponsorships are coming, that a certain post is sponsored, etc. Most readers will be excited for you, but some hate advertisements. A quick warning is usually enough to keep them happy.

Also try to avoid negative sponsorships, where you simply bash a company you don't like (maybe because it turned down your sponsorship request?). This sort of behavior is small-minded and petty, and not a good tone to set on your blog.   It will also decrease your chances of every receiving sponsorship from any other company.   If you are afraid that a legitimate sponsor just wants to use your blog to write negative things about someone or something else, it is probably best to turn down that offer, too, no matter how good the money might be.

However, most of these concerns will never come up. Sponsorships can be a really exciting way to earn a little money, help out readers, and maybe even draw in some new readership.

Tip from Jill -

We have already briefly talked about sponsorships. It really is as easy as reaching out and asking.

Chapter 43 - Advertorial

The internet is full of made up words – "tweeting" was something birds did and let's not even start to list all the acronyms on blogs, Facebook, and Twitter. So there is no reason to be intimidated by the term "advertorial." It is simply a combination of advertisement and editorial.

The "advertisement" part of the word is pretty easy. You are allowing a company to post something on your blog in exchange for money. So where does "editorial" play in? An editorial is a section of the newspaper that, originally, allowed the editor of the paper to write about his own views and opinions. Modern editorials also feature "guest" writers (sometimes mayors or celebrities). So in this situation, think of the editorial portion as an opinion.

Whose opinion? Yours! That's right, you get to post about your opinion of a product and get paid to do it – that is an advertorial. Of course, the catch is that you are probably going to be required to post something positive about the product. But, it also means you'll not only get money, but a free sample to try.

Advertorials are a lot like sponsorships, in that a company will be paying you to say something nice about their business or product. While sponsorships may provide you with an advertisement or logo that you are required to post on your blog, the advertorial can be written in your own words (although the company might want to see it before it goes live).

So how can you let businesses know you're open to advertorials? It is easy – you just have to tell them. The same departments that deal with sponsorships will probably also be open to advertorial suggestions (or suggest them themselves if you ask for a sponsorship).

If you're interested in doing an advertorial (or many), find a product or products you love and just start writing. These can be great samples to send out to businesses that you are not only serious about their product, but ready to post something positive about them immediately. If your blog is dedicated to reviewing products, you might even come under their radar before you write a single word about their product.

As with sponsorships, you probably want to let your readers know you're getting paid to rave about a product, just for ethical purposes, but for the most part, people are interested to hear about what you have to say – especially if they are already reading your blog.

Advertorials are definitely a route to travel when monetizing your blog.

Tip from Pinal -

Advertorials are a way of pointing out the companies you like and admire. You can reach out to companies, or write the advertorial first and see if they're willing to compensate you.

Chapter 44 - Affiliate marketing

Depending on what type of blog you are writing, you might be all set up to sell products on your website.   It might be something you started out interested in doing, or it might be something that has recently become an interest after years of just blogging. No matter what subject matter your blog is about, chances are there is some product that you could sell that your readers would be interested in buying.

However, starting selling items and starting a business like this can be complicated.   You not only have to decide what product to sell, but you may also have to be in charge of producing, designing and manufacturing these products.   At some point, you might have to decide if the money you make off the sales of this product will pay for the time you invested in all these decisions.

This is not to scare you away from selling things on your blog.   If you are just interested in selling T-shirts and mugs with your logo on them, it is probably not going to be as hard as I made it sound.   But if you want to expand and sell more complex products – or a product that already exists that you would simply like to provide your readers easy access to, affiliate marketing is something to consider.

Affiliate marketing means that you team up with another company with a product to sell, and you sell it on your blog for a cut of the profits. This can be a niche market type of product that the owner doesn't know how to sell, or it can be an extremely popular product, but one that your readers are interested in buying (and why not earn a little profit while providing the service?). There are a million different products you could sell, and a million different ways to earn money through affiliate marketing.

You can earn a simple percentage of the profits, or you can earn a dollar amount based on units sold. You might have to buy a bulk amount of the product, and mark it up for sale on your website in order to make a profit. You may simply provide a link to the product on your blog, but earn money per click. The way you earn money will differ from product to product and company to company. The important thing is to be comfortable with the profit margin and be happy with your new partnership.

So how to you find an affiliate to market with? As with most monetizing options, you just have to check. Large companies will have departments devoted to these requests, to you, might just have to ask around to see if anyone is looking to sell an item. Some partnerships may arise naturally, when you hear someone has a product and you are a willing blog.

Affiliate marketing is usually not a monetizing option that is going to fall into your lap – it is something you will have to do some research on and go out searching for. But if you are interested in making a little money, this is definitely an option.

Tip from Jill -

Affiliate marketing is a way of selling items on your blog that you don't have to manufacture yourself. It's a win-win situation for you and the affiliate.

Chapter 45 - Products

We have already danced around the idea of selling products on your blog. We have mentioned sponsorships and affiliate marketing. We talked about selling products on your blog in our monetizing introduction. Selling items on your blog might be the easiest way to monetize your blog, though, and the one you can control the most.

Selling a product on your blog is going back to the roots of the business. The first person to start a business wasn't allowing advertising on their cave painting – they were selling a product (probably bartering some meat for some grains, or similar). So if the idea of selling products on your blog scares you a little bit, just remember that if the cavemen could do it, you can too.

First step – determine what you would like to sell. As mentioned before, there is no reason to be super fancy. You can stick with branded t-shirts and mugs at first. These are probably the easiest things to sell and the easiest to make (there are hundreds of companies online, where you can just upload your image, and have a case shipped to you with that logo plastered all over the item of your choosing). Obviously you may have ideas beyond t-shirts and mugs, but this is just an easy place to start and an easy example.

Next – determine how to sell them on your blog. Many blogging platforms have widgets or tools that let you post your product on the blog itself with all the important "buy," "cart," and "check out" buttons. Alternatively, you may just need to provide a link to your eBay store on your blog.

Third step – let people know! Write a blog post about the new items that you are selling. Put it on your social media sites. Don't beg people to buy, just let them know the option is there.

Last step – profit! Well, at least let's hope you profit. If you even sell one item, which is more than you did before. Keep track of your best-selling items, and pay attention to what the feedback you get from your buyers. Some items will be more popular than others, for no reason that you could have anticipated. Think of it as part of the fun of monetizing your blog.

Selling products on your blog is not difficult. It is even easier than using AdSense, because you have complete control over *what* you sell, *where* you advertise it, and *how often* you talk about the products. If you are interested in monetizing your blog, this is a step I highly recommend.

Tip from Pinal -

Blogs have many opportunities for monetizing that traditional businesses do not have. But they can also be traditional – a marketplace to sell your own product.

Chapter 46 - Services

We've talked about a lot of ways to monetize your blog so far. I have tried to keep this advice as generalized as possible because I know that the types of blogs are so widespread that ONE rule is not going to apply to everyone. Blogs can be about everything from artistic photographs to one type of programming language. The ways to monetize those two blogs are going to be very different.

This chapter is about services. This is one of those topics that is not going to be useful to everyone. If you are just blogging funny pictures of your cat dressed up in outfits, you might not have a service you can market on your blog. OR you can sell your skills as a pet photographer, funny photo stager, or advice about how to get a cat to sit still while wearing a hat. So no matter what your blog is about, please consider that services might be an option for you.

So I just mentioned a few services that can be provided – advice, an e-book about skills, or selling your time to help others with a similar problem. There are many variations on this theme, and if you are blogging because you an expert about something, you are probably already thinking of examples for your own blog.

Marketing your services on your blog is going to look really similar to selling a product. First, put it on your blog! You can use the same type of layout if you were selling a physical product, with the "buy," "cart" and "check out" buttons. A link to eBay may not work with services, but you can still accept payment for services on PayPal.

Next, let people know. Write a post about how you are going to be providing consulting services, or are willing to come out and help individuals with their own cat photography (for example) for $XX per hour. Announce it on Facebook and Twitter, or your social media of choice.

Third step – profit! No, this isn't a joke this time. Because services are just a matter of providing your time, which you didn't have to pay for in the first place, *any* money you make by providing your services is going to be pure profit.

Services are an amazing way to monetize your blog. I cannot recommend them highly enough. You can control the way they are marketed on your blog, in the same way as products, and there is also a lot less overhead investment required. You might not think services are something you can provide – I hope this chapter changed your mind (or at least made you think twice).

Tip from Jill -

If your blog is about "advice" and "tips and tricks" more than "products," providing your services to monetize your blog.

Chapter 47 - Built-to-Sell Blogs

Starting a small business might be one of the riskiest propositions in today's modern market. Large "big box" stores have made the market extremely competitive, and small businesses have a hard time keeping up. With that said – starting a blog is kind of like starting a small business. You will be competing with hugely popular blogs (the Wal-Mart of blogs, if you will) and you will feel very much like a small fish in a big pond.

There is another over-lap between blogs and businesses. When someone starts their own business, eventually they are going to have to face the future of their company – do they want to stay small forever? Do they want to grow up into a jumbo chain store? Do they want to sell and retire on the profits?

When you start a blog, you might just be looking for somewhere to write down your thoughts. But eventually, you will have to ask yourself about the future of your blog. Do you want to retire on the profits from monetizing? Would you like to become a huge player in the blogging world? Is this a temporary adventure, and eventually you'd like to transition to something else? Or would you like to sell your blog for money?

That's right, blogs can be sold just like a business. If you are very lucky (and popular) you might even be able to retire on the proceeds, just like someone who sold their business. Now, I wish that I could give you a step-by-step rule book about how to make a blog that is "built-to-sell." Obviously this is impossible. I have no knowledge or control over the type of blog you write, the kind of readers who will visit, the kind of buyers you'll attract, and the kind of profit to expect. These variables are as impossible to predict as a breeze.

I am including this as a "monetize your blog" subject because it is definitely an option to keep in mind, and it is definitely a way to make money on your blog. There is no rule of thumb to follow regarding pricing, so this is something that has to be learned as you go.

The best way to ensure that you will make money from the sale of a blog is to write a blog that is built to sell. This means pin-pointing an extremely popular topic, and writing a perfectly tailored blog about it. You can begin marketing a blog this this almost from day one.

I cannot over-emphasize the fact that if you are blogging about something you love, there is no guarantee that you can sell it and retire as a millionaire – but that's probably not the reason why you started the blog, is it?

Tip from Pinal -

If you want, blogs can be sold to investors the same way a business can be sold. You can even design your blog to be sold from the very start.

Chapter 48 - Frequent Poster, Wide Variety Blogs

We set out to write a book about blogging that would cover the wide world of blogging, but was not hundreds of pages long and too intimidating to beginning bloggers. The decision was to make sure the book only had about chapters, that way a person could read one post each week and learn to blog in a year (or quicker if they so desired). We are quickly reaching the end already. We have covered a lot of topics, from starting a blog, to monetizing it, choosing a platform to deciding on your comments section. It has been a lot of information to absorb.

Now we would like to put all this information together, and show actual examples to illustrate some of my points. We are going to stick with "big name" blogs, because choosing a favorite "smaller" blog is much, much too difficult (and I don't want to look like I'm choosing favorites, when really I just don't have enough room to do everyone justice!).

Right now, I'd like to show a few blogs that post a lot of articles, often multiple posts a day, and cover a wide variety of topics. These examples are mostly going to be news style blogs, because the news is always changing and will represent the best kind of "frequent poster, wide variety" examples I am thinking of.

http://technorati.com/

This blog focuses on, you might have guessed, technology.   It has a great design, and is almost constantly updated by a team of bloggers. It focuses mostly on breaking tech news, with some opinion pieces and reviews thrown in.

http://digg.com/

This is a collection of news articles from almost all the news outlets from around the world. There is not a lot of original material – most of the material has been submitted by the news outlets themselves, or voted on by readers (who link from an article to Digg using an icon on most websites next to the social media icons). While it isn't a blog in the sense that there is one person writing all the content, it is a good example of how varied the definition of "blog" can be!

http://www.cheezburger.com/

This is a collection of humorous websites (the many, many varieties can be found at the tabs along the top of the page). It's complete silliness and lack of serious material is only outweighed by the fact that it is extremely popular, and one of the most visited humor websites on the internet. It started simply as funny cat photos, created by bloggers and submitted by readers (the name comes from a photo of sad cat, with the caption "I can haz Cheezburger?") and ballooned into a comedy giant.

http://gawker.com/

This is another not-very-serious websites, whose various branches focus mainly on gossip. It started as a traditional blog, and is another blog that ballooned into many branches with many paid bloggers providing almost 24-7 content.

These are just a few examples of extremely prolific blogs. You might be happy to get one post out a day, and feel intimidated by blogs this size. Please keep in mind that ALL these sites have teams of bloggers, writing and submitting every day. But these blogs are all also good examples of how one small idea can grow into a giant blogging company.

Tip from Jill -

Take a look at these examples to find ways to design your blog for frequent posts and updates. Pay attention to layout and color usage.

Chapter 49 - Infrequent Posting, Highly Topical Blogs

We started this book, trying to write 52 chapters about blogging. We have almost reached that goal. The breadth of the information we covered might have been completely overwhelming, so now I am trying to show some examples of bloggers who "made it."

I am going to stick with well known, popular blogs, because choosing smaller blogs is just too difficult – I love too many! I am also afraid that if I tried to share every single blog I love, I would run out of the room, or have to start another giant book called "My Favorite Blogs."

So here are some generic examples of blogs with very narrow subjects. They post a little less frequently than the larger blogs I highlighted in the last chapter, but some still do post multiple articles a day (just 5, instead of 50). Don't let this intimidate you, as a beginning blogger, someday you might have teams of writers working for you, just like these blogs do.

http://www.wired.com/

This is the blog associated with the tech magazine, Wired. While they still post original material daily, they are generally smaller news articles. The main articles are posted around the same time line as the print magazine. This magazine focuses on computers, software, hardware, and other (self-proclaimed) geeky subjects.

http://www.problogger.net/

I feel this blog is pertinent to this whole book – it is a blog about how to become the best blogger ever. They follow their own advice and post often, but not nearly at the same rate as some of the news blogs, for example. You won't find a lot of reviews or gossip here, it is almost 100% blogging advice, 100% of the time.

http://www.macworld.com/

This is another blog associated with a print magazine (MacWorld). Like Wired, it comes out with most of its articles concurrently with its print issues. You might have guessed from the name, this blog focuses on news, reviews, and gossip regarding Apple computers.

http://boingboing.net/

This is a somewhat more obscure blog that focuses its posts on science and technology. It also has a team of bloggers and guest contributors who talk about the most recent news, research, and developments in the sciences – biology, chemistry, physics, astronomy, even computer science.

While this list might show my personal bias (technology and science), I think they are still good examples for would-be-bloggers, no matter what you want your niche to be.

Tip from Pinal -

These blogs are great examples of blogs with less frequent posting, but good layout to catch the eye and keep readers engaged.

Chapter 50 - Great Blog Design

Almost a year ago, we started writing this book.   I knew that blogging was a large enough topic that it would take us a year to cover – and believe me, I could keep going for another year!   But I think it is time to turn off the fire hose of information, and start looking at real world examples.

I have been sticking with the "big name" blogs in these chapters because, trust me, I have too many favorite blogs to count.   I could feature a favorite blog once a week for years!   So I am choosing blogs that you have probably heard about, or even read, and hoping that you take a look at them with fresh eyes and think "I can do that."

In the chapters about blog design, I'm sure many of you were feeling a little scared, maybe kind of bored, and I'm sure a lot of you thought "I'll deal with that later."   I think that the following examples will help you tie everything together, and even give you a few ideas.

http://www.cheezburger.com/

This blog is one of the most basic (even though it is technically a huge website).   Notice that it is simply in reverse chronological order, and you could scroll down the page looking at funny pictures, hitting the "next" button, for ages. Information about the company is right up top, including links to "sister" blogs, and other information is arranged down the sidebar. Really, despite how much is going on this site, it is a pretty bare-bones layout.

http://www.wired.com/

Wired has a little bit of a fancier layout, but don't let it overwhelm you. The most popular articles (or the ones they want to be the most popular) are right up top, and hard *not* to click on. Other articles are arranged below. If you keep scrolling, you'll see lists of older articles divided up by categories – what you're really looking at is blog post archives. Really, the fancy photos and links is what makes this blog look so flashy. You can have a layout like this, too!

http://www.theverge.com/

The Verge is a website about pop culture – its bloggers write about what everyone is talking about, no matter the topic – politics, sports, technology, culture, movies, the list could go on (and it does, on the blog). It also sports a pretty fancy layout. Popular articles of the day are laid out in tiles, and as you scroll down you'll see that each day's article are grouped in repeating tiled patterns. Having a design like this requires the skills of a graphic designer – but it can be done!

http://boingboing.net/

Boing Boing has a slightly "backwards" layout. It feels pretty familiar at first, because it has a simple scrolling layout (reverse chronological order). But you'll notice that other articles are also scrolling along the left sidebar (usually things are on the right sidebar, and don't scroll along with you, but stay static). This is another "looks fancy, but easy to achieve" layout, and works well for news article-style sites, maybe because it is reminiscent of a newspaper layout.

Tip from Jill -

Not every blog has to be a standard "posts down to the middle, right-hand side bar" layout. These blogs demonstrate many different blog layouts available.

Chapter 51 - Big Money Maker Blogs

So far, we have written, and you have read, more than 50 chapters about how to become a blogger, and/or make your blog better. It has been a lot of information to digest, and we barely scraped the surface! I could write for another whole year about the technical details of blogging.

I think that at some point, though, a good teacher *shows* not just *tells*. So I am going to show some examples of some of the principles we have discussed. You will probably recognize most of the blogs I mention, and I do that for a reason. If I mentioned every one of my favorite smaller blogs, this book would stretch into a dictionary-style directory of blogs, and that sounds like too much work, even for me!

One of our last topics (before these example chapters) was about monetizing blogs. Some of you might have rolled your eyes at the idea, but I am going to give some examples right now of blogs that monetized successfully, and eventually sold for a lot (think millions) of dollars. Some of these are names you will recognize, and some you will think "who would pay a million dollars for that?" Wouldn't it be nice if your blog ended up on the "who would pay a million dollars for that?" list?

www.Techcrunch.com

TechCrunch was a blog that was dedicated to all things tech. It was founded in 2005 by Michael Arrington – yes, a single blogger with his own niche blog. And it sold in 2011 for $30 million. This is, of course, the ultimate dream for most bloggers, and is certainly not the rule. But in a time when geeky things like technology blogs were *not* the norm, one blogger made a life-changing profits.

www.Arstechnica.com

Ars Technica is another example of a blog founded by a single blogger. Ken Fisher founded the blog in 1998, and established himself as an expert in all things technological. A decade later, publishing giant Conde Nast bought the blog for $25 million.

www.Livejournal.com

This can be considered more of a blogging platform, but it is still a success story. Founded in 1999, it sold eight years later for $25 million.

www.Babyrazzi.com

This is an example of a niche blog that didn't seem destined for millions. It is a website that publishes photos of celebrities' babies (the name is a combination of "baby" and "paparazzi"). This doesn't seem like an obvious money making scheme, but four years after

Danielle Friedland started her blog, she sold it to Times, Inc for $10 million.

www.Gardenrant.com

This is a blog about gardening – that is it. Susan Harris started a blog about her garden in 1996 (when the internet was still almost brand new!). In 2007, she sold it for $1.3 million. Now, that's not as much as the highest ranked blog on this list, but would you turn your nose up at $1.3 million? I didn't think so. Now get out there and start blogging!

Tip from Pinal -

Selling your blog for millions of dollars might be a one-in-a-million experience, but these examples are meant to inspire you to greatness!

Chapter 52 - In Conclusion

When we started this book, we weren't sure who the target audience should be – beginners or experts? Who needed the most advice? Who do we want to talk to? I have been blogging for more than ten years myself, and I am not ashamed to admit that I learned things while writing this book. I hope that many of you learned along with me.

This is a bittersweet chapter for me to write, because I really enjoyed writing this book. It was fun to learn, it was fun to teach, and it was fun to pass along to people and image how it can make their own blogging as enjoyable as I find mine. I am sorry that the book is over, but proud of what we all have accomplished here.

I also thought a long time about how to finish a book with such a wide subject matter. What huge advice could I save up for the end, and really blow everyone's mind with my final chapter? What tip could I give that is sure to make all my readers wealthy, happy, and successful? Obviously, when I put these sort of standards up for myself, I was feeling very hesitant about succeeding.

I am happy to announce, though, that I think I found the *perfect* piece of advice to finish this book with a bang. Please, everyone, think of a drum-roll in your head while I announce the BEST blogging advice, in the history of blogging: Love What You Do.

That's right – if you are writing a niche blog about cat photography, muffin baking, soap sculpture carving, or whatever crazy hobby you're in, and it is what gets you out of bed with a smile every morning, you have found a successful blog. It doesn't matter if you're not monetized, or you don't have a social media presence. If you are genuinely happy just to be writing words and posting them on the internet, you are a successful blogger.

Of course, when you're this happy, you probably want to share it with the world. That's why you're putting it on the internet, after all. That is the whole point of this whole book, and I hope that everyone understands that. If you love what you do, you don't need to do SEO. But SEO can help you find others out there who love soap sculpture carving just as much as you do.

Personally, I think I have found my calling in blogging. I get out of bed every day with a smile. I wrote this book hoping that I could spread that joy around. I truly believe that if you love what you do, other good things will follow.

If you believe the same thing – let me know. You can find my contact info at my own blog, http://blog.sqlauthority.com.   Email me or leave a comment, and tell me your stories, I would love to hear them. If you also have questions, feel free to ask them, I will try to help spread the joy!

Tip from Pinal -

If you do what you love, you'll love what you do. Blogging can be a way to make a living, but if you love every minute of it, it won't feel like work.

"Live as if your were to die tomorrow. Learn as if you were to live forever."

~Mahatma Gandhi

Continue the journey

http://blog.sqlauthority.com

http://www.facebook.com/SQLAuth

Secret Tool Box of Successful Bloggers

52 Tips to Build a High Traffic Top Ranking Blog

Pinal Dave

Pinal is an eternal learner and avid technology blogger. He has authored 11 books and built 15 e-learning video courses with Pluralsight. He has been a part of the IT industry for more than ten years and works for Pluralsight. He received his Master of Science from the University of Southern California and a Bachelors of Engineering from Gujarat University. Additionally, he holds many Microsoft certificates.

Pinal writes every day on his blog http://blog.sqlauthority.com for over 8 years on various subjects concerning SQL, NoSQL, and Business Intelligence. His blog has over million visitors every month and he is known for engaging users with his skills of explaining a complex subject in simple words. When he is not in front of a computer, he is usually travelling to explore hidden treasures in nature with his daughter, Shaivi, and very supportive wife, Nupur.

Jillian Gile

Jillian has been writing and editing blogs for five years. She currently is a freelance writer and a guest blogger for a variety of websites. She has her Master of Science in Biology from Washington State Univerisity. When Jillian is not writing, she is a Research Scientist for the Univeristy of Washington.